ROXBURY LIBRARY

For Hans Baldwin
for Old Times Sake
W. G. H.

March 1987

MUSINGS AND REMINISCENCES OF A PSEUDO-SCIENTIST

MUSINGS AND REMINISCENCES OF A PSEUDO-SCIENTIST

JOHN EAGER HOWARD

Exposition Press of Florida, Inc.• Pompano Beach, Florida

FIRST EDITION

© 1985 by John Eager Howard

All rights reserved. No part of this book may be reproduced in whole or in part, in any form or by any means, electronic or mechanical, including photyocopying, recording, or by any information storage and retrieval system, without permission in writing from the publisher. Address inquiries to Exposition Press of Florida, 1701 Blount Road, Pompano Beach, FL 33069.

ISBN 0-682-40260-5

Printed in the United States of America

Contents

Foreword	vii
Birth and Early Years	1
Hill School	3
Princeton	6
Medical School	9
Boston	16
Early Hopkins Postgraduate Years	21
The Osler Service Years (1930–1932)	24
War Years	29
Macy Meetings Under the Auspices of OSRD	32
The Privilege of Caring for Dr. Edwards A. Park	33
The Post-War Years	37
Studies on Urinary Stones	40
The Phosphate Story	41
Private Practice	42
Personal Medical Problems	45
Guy's Hospital	48
Hurricanes	52
Trip to Mexico	54
Changes in Johns Hopkins and Baltimore	56

Foreword

At a recent trial, Dr. John Eager Howard was called to give expert testimony on a case involving the diagnosis of an endocrine disorder. An attorney is reported to have begun questioning him by asking, "Dr. Howard, you are an endocrinologist?" "No," replied Dr. Howard, to the astonishment of the attorney and the court. "You're not an endocrinologist?" persisted the attorney. "No," said Dr. Howard, "I am a physician."

Dr. Howard is indeed a physician, first and foremost. For many years he has been on the staffs of The Johns Hopkins Hospital and The Union Memorial Hospital. This role has been inextricably linked to his teaching and investigation as Professor of Medicine at The Johns Hopkins University School of Medicine. Many medical students and residents have come under his tutelage, and some forty fellows have studied and worked under his direction.

In 1947, when Dr. Howard offered me a fellowship and I accepted, he shot back a one-word telegram, "Swell." Over the years I have come to recognize that his succinctness of expression is a product of his thoroughness of thought. A master clinician and scientist, always seeking perfection in himself, John Howard also expects the best from his fellows and shows sore disappointment in medical students and residents if their work is slipshod. Equally, however, he shows satisfaction when his own investigations add a new dimension to medical knowledge, and he takes pride in the accomplishment of his associates and students. His patients, many of whom are referred to him with puzzling illnesses, appreciate his keen mind and accept his occasionally brusque but always incisive questioning on their symptoms. In turn, they win his loyalty and affection; he often brings them flowers or berries from his garden, a book from his library or oysters from the market.

My words cannot fully capture the essence of the man. Fortunately, however, autobiography is authentic biography, and in this splendid volume Dr. Howard tells of his interesting eighty years and of the events that have shaped his career. He omits, probably out of modesty, some honors that have come his way, such as the presidency of the Endocrine Society, his membership in the Association of American Physicians, and a Chair of Medicine at Johns Hopkins recently established in his name.

With a devotion to duty and service like that of his illustrious great-great-grandfather and namesake, John Eager Howard has added to the advancement and betterment of humankind. We who know him and those who may come to know him in the reading of this book, in our attempt to emulate him and echo his crisp style, can say only, "Thanks."

Samuel P. Asper, M.D.

July, 1984

MUSINGS AND REMINISCENCES OF A PSEUDO-SCIENTIST

Birth and Early Years

A biographical sketch should begin with the date and place of birth of the subject. I was born August 27, 1902, in the "Poor House," in Greenspring Valley of Baltimore County. The Poor House does not connote an "alms house" but was the residence of a Mr. Poor, which has since become the main building of the Garrison Forest School for Girls. In those days it was not uncommon for residents of Baltimore City to rent county estates for two or three months in summer and move their families to more salubrious air.

There emerges here an incident, one of the more amusing of my life, when some 75 years later I was applying for Medicare at the appropriate government office. The lady administrator behind the desk asked the place and date of my birth and was answered as stated above. She looked somewhat aghast but continued her writing. Having then told her I was not aware of possessing a birth certificate, her next question was could I get hold of the obstetrician present at my birth and perhaps he could vouch that I had indeed been born. My face indicated such astonishment at this suggestion that finally she too burst out laughing. A church baptismal record was finally found and I was successfully awarded my Medicare card.

My memory of succeeding years until school attendance is very hazy. We lived on Lanvale Street in northwestern Baltimore in a house set well back on a shaded green lawn. A trolley car trudged its way up the steep hill of Park Avenue to Lanvale Street, then to McMechen Street and eastward across the North Avenue Bridge, which was the northern boundary of the city. Charles Street was the end of the line and at the northeast corner of this junction was a rambling old building known as the University School for Boys, headed by a superlative teacher, Mr. William Marston. To this seat of learning I was trundled at age six for the learning of the three

R's, to remain until fourteen years old. At first I was escorted to school on the trolley but soon was sent off alone to walk the mile and a half with books under my arm.

I recall too few exciting events at the school but, to my everlasting rejoicing, I was superbly indoctrinated into Latin by Mr. Marston himself. The morning classes were broken by a walk about a quarter-mile down Charles Street to the Baltimore Athletic Club where we wrestled, ran, swam and did calisthenics until a walk back to school for lunch. The athletics program was small; a trolley was taken to Mount Washington certain afternoons where football was instructed.

The boys approximately my age were a fine lot, many going on to distinguished careers. Among them were Howard K. Gray, who became an All-American end in football at Princeton, and a famed Mayo Clinic surgeon; James Bordley, who had a distinguished career in medicine, and the Middendorf twins, who were on the Harvard crew which won at Henley on the Thames in 1917. Many did not finish their undergraduate days at Marston's, being sent away to boarding schools at about fourteen years of age, as was I.

The boys in my neighborhood not attending Marston's were also an unusual lot. Usually in off hours we roller-skated on the recently asphalt-paved street and played hockey. Not too badly, either, except we could never skate nearly so gracefully as could the black boys in our environment, who were as graceful on rollers as our professional ice skaters are today. I recall no racial problems in those days, though we did not compete directly then with any of our black compatriots.

Among the neighbors who later had distinguished careers were William L. Marbury, Jr., who became head of the Harvard Corporation; Hanson Baldwin, who was chief war correspondent for the New York Times; Richard Shackelford, with a distinguished athletic career at Princeton, and later a surgical career; McLane Fisher, prominent architect, as well as many others.

Our households were run in a much similar form to one another. My three sisters, two older and one younger, insisted that I was spoiled but it seemed to me that they nearly always had the best of it. My father, who somehow felt German would be the language of the future, always had German girls known as fräuleins to look after the affairs of my sisters. Until well past the inception of school,

German was always spoken in the presence of the fräuleins, whose presence I resented. An elderly black woman named Louisa, who had been born a slave on my great-grandfather's place but after freedom chose to live with us, was by her choice and mine assigned to look after me. I recall I would let no one else turn off the gaslight at bedtime but Louisa, and was always rewarded with a good head scratch. I loved Louisa very dearly and was heartbroken when she died at age 90 in a home for the aged, called in those days a shelter. Nearly every Sunday afternoon my father would walk with me the few blocks to her "home."

There was always a black butler who did not live in but came early in the morning to stoke the furnace, and an Irish cook who daily made the lightest and crispiest rolls I can recall, unless there were corn or buckwheat cakes. Sundays we always had sausage and buckwheat cakes from Thanksgiving to Easter, when an abrupt change in menus was made to kidney stew and waffles. For syrup on buckwheat cakes, my father insisted on "blackstrap" molasses, and woe betide anyone who poured on maple syrup, as my sisters and mother frequently did. There was a maid to do the rooms and general housecleaning, and a laundress who came by the day, who rounded out the establishment.

Hill School

My reasons for ending up at the Hill School in Pottstown, Pennsylvania, resulted from my Presbyterian mother's friendship with our minister, Reverend Maltbie Babcock. My parents escorted me by rail to the august hills of Pennsylvania and presented me to Mrs. John Meigs, widow of the Hill School's founder. Here, for the first month, I spent my most miserable days. Each new student was assigned to a senior who would "look after" him, but knowing no one at the school at all, a more homesick boy never existed. Roommates were soon changed, which helped somewhat, but it must have been six months or more, when I adapted to new methods of study and instruction, that things began to look up. I had been forced to drop back a year in class, which provided some advantage in grades. One had specific hours of study hall, two to three hours at a stretch, but if one attained a grade 1 or 2 average, the privilege of studying in the room was allowed. This became quickly discernible and I never had "study hall" after the first two months.

Discipline was strict; lateness was a sin of the first order. One was wakened early by loud bells, early breakfast, chapel, and classes began at 8:30. Athletics for the lower school were regulated. I was assigned in my first spring to play baseball on a "little team." One incident occurred which I shall never forget, unpleasant though it was. An infield fly ball was hit near second base. I was playing shortstop, thought the ball was mine but the second baseman came over and deflected it with his fingers, the ball landing plumb on my eye. Fortunately the eye was not injured but the resulting hematoma was a sight to behold. I was immediately dispatched to the infirmary, where during the night the eye completely closed and a hematoma appeared about the size of the baseball which had caused it. Dr. Wylie, the school physician, arranged for a box of leeches to be sent up from Philadelphia and my sensations of the next few days were extraordinary. A tiny nick was made in the skin and a leech applied. With rhythmic suction the leech became engorged and another would be applied. After about a week, the leeches had done their job. I could see out of the eye and return to classes—notorious but hardly famous—but what an experience!

In upper class years I became a tennis devotee and, though small for that game, became fairly adept. I played on the school teams for three years (Hill School was rarely beaten in tennis in those days), reached the final of the Princeton interscholastics in senior year and was team captain as well as being awarded the school cup. In those days William Tatum Tilden was just coming into his heyday. He enjoyed teaching lads and was a frequent visitor at Hill School, teaching and coaching the game. On occasion, the week after school was out, he would invite four or five of us from around the Philadelphia district to be his guests for a week of tennis at the Germantown Cricket Club. These were indeed strenuous days—tennis from morn to night, techniques, strategy, and just about everything. If one flinched when slapped a hard forehand for you to volley, woebetide you, and if the racquet head was not always held higher than the handle on a volley, the very devil broke loose. There, though I met many of Tilden's later pupils—Arnold Jones, Charlie Watson and others—I never saw, nor did they, any hint of the problems which later involved Tilden in disgrace.

For a while in my fourth form year, we roomed adjacent to Ralph Hills, a giant of a man even at 14, who became one of my closest friends for life. Because he had short-cropped black, stubby hair over a large skull, I christened him "Bruno" because he reminded me of the south end of a bear cub walking north. The name stuck and Bruno Hills became world famous not only as an outstanding track athlete, placing in the Olympic shot put event, but an excellent internist in Baltimore.

My next three years at the Hill, I shared a room with William Draper Blair of Silver Spring, Maryland. This companionship lasted through all four years at Princeton. A perfect gentleman of the old school, quiet, thoughtful, kindly, a friend I still admire mightily, Bill Blair had many siblings and a most wonderful mother who had us as houseguests at her homes in Silver Spring and Hyannisport, and took us on innumerable gay (not in the current sense) trips in her chauffeured Locomobile. Bill's father had been invalided by a horrendous combat with malaria, with survival from an alleged fever of 109°. However, he was still able to get about a bit, but spent long hours at a card table playing Russian Bank, in solitaire if necessary. He enjoyed hugely teaching the game to others and Bill and I spent many happy hours with him at the card table. Mr. Blair also taught me to like Potomac roe herring for breakfast, a delicacy repugnant to many persons, and which, while cooking, provides an aroma that invariably pervades the whole house.

Bill Blair played on the Princeton baseball team and, incidentally, later became President of the Bank of Silver Spring. It should perhaps be mentioned here that during our freshman year at

Princeton, Bill Blair and I had taken a third roommate, one Charles Douglas Jackson, above whom I slept that first year in a double decker iron bed. Jackson, who had also matriculated at Hill School, was a brilliant student, spoke perfect French (he had a French mother) and was instrumental, along with John Martin and Parker Lloyd-Smith, in helping found *Time, Fortune* and *Life* magazines. Later he became an advisor to President Eisenhower, lived in the White House, and created a sensation at our 25th wedding anniversary by arriving in a Presidential chauffeur-driven limousine.

At Hill School I was most fortunately selected as one of twelve students to be taught Greek by that Mr. Chips of American school teachers, Mr. Alfred Rolfe. Two or three of those students received grades of 100 on the college board examination in Greek, and I was never sure that Mr. Rolfe had not been on the grading committee. Nevertheless, four Hill School classmates from Mr. Rolfe's course continued Greek during our four years at Princeton, and we rather smugly felt that we knew more than did our instructors. We also continued Latin through Princeton, and I have never regretted those hours spent on ancient languages, though nowadays such is not considered an ideal education for a prospective physician.

Princeton

I sailed through Princeton, having a wonderful time with no thought for the future. An incident occurred early in my sophomore year that greatly embarrassed me. In July, 1921, the combined Princeton and Stanford University tennis teams played Oxford and Cambridge in a team match. I was allowed to play because by that time freshman year had ended. At the very close of my match on a very hot day I developed leg cramps and was, quite illegally, massaged for some five minutes on the court from which I could not rise. I was allowed to resume play and I always felt the courteous Englishman purposely lost that match, for he did not return a single service, which ended the match. Later that fall a pep rally was held before a big football game and the dean of Princeton gave a speech. The dean had been present at Seabright during that tennis match and eulogized my spirit on the occasion and commended it as an example for Princeton athletes. I was not present at the gathering but was taunted no end by others who were, much to my embarrassment.

A great deal of my time at Princeton was spent on the tennis courts. The freshman team, of which I was a member, took on all comers with success for which we received our straight numerals (without the TT underneath). It was felt by most of us that we could trim the varsity, but all challenges for such a test were refused. While practicing one day in freshman year, I saw, to my horror, my first view of an epileptic seizure. The player began suddenly to thrash about with arms and legs, fell to the ground and had guttural rumblings. None of us had the remotest notion of what was going on, and so did nothing but observe. Soon Aydelotte, who later made the freshman team but then dropped out of college, came to and told us all about his having had previous attacks but that they occurred sporadically. But he never again that year had a similar episode while playing tennis.

The following year the tennis varsity was unusually strong, without individual giants, but the first and sixth members were almost evenly matched. Since scoring was one point for each match played, we won nearly all the third, fourth, fifth and sixth matches, taking the Eastern title and the privilege of wearing an unadorned orange P on a black sweater, and becoming members of the Varsity Club. A little trinket displaying a gold tiger, worn on the watch chain, permitted one free admission to all athletic contests except the major football games. As a senior I captained the team but did not win all my matches by any means and got only to the quarterfinals in the National Intercollegiates. But in junior year, right after the close of the season, I came to Baltimore and won the Maryland State Open Tournament. This was considerably eased by a favorable draw, for nearly all collegiate players, even from the far West, were participants to tune up for the Intercollegiates soon to follow. For this achievement the reward was a small silver cigarette box, on which now the name and date are almost obliterated from frequent polishing.

During my Princeton years I had become friendly with Dean Mathey, a former Intercollegiate doubles champion while at Princeton and currently a partner in the New York brokerage firm of Dillon Read. Mathey made frequent excursions from New York and often played with members of the team. As noted above, I had been sailing through Princeton quite oblivious of the future but vaguely expecting to join my father's brokerage firm in some capacity. Dean Mathey offered me a job with Dillon Read to learn the business and draw a small salary while so doing.

During Christmas vacation, at breakfast one morning, I told my father of this possibility. His reaction was one of astonishing wrath. Apparently his view of this New York firm was rather dim and he said in no uncertain terms that if I followed that line, I could never have any part of his banking firm. What to do? I was aware that the family would have liked to see me become a parson, but my self-evaluation in such a post did not seem favorable. The family had great admiration for several physicians—Doctors Finney, Thayer, and Knox, among others. So I said to my father, "How would you like me to go to medical school?" His reply was instantaneous: "I'll pay your way through."

But what did one do to get *into* medical school? Father arranged for an appointment with Dr. Whitridge Williams, an old school friend, who was then Dean of the Johns Hopkins Medical School. My meeting with Dr. Williams was in some ways ludicrous, and I doubt whether such a meeting would ever happen today, the way medical schools are run. He viewed my Princeton credentials with the recurrent comment that the marks were adequate but the choice of courses for a medical career seemed bizarre. "Conklin's course in Biology and McLanahan's course in Physics will serve you in good stead, but why all the ancient languages?" He then handed me a paper in French, on which I did all right, and then asked what *eiweiss* was. That being white of egg, Dr. Williams sank comfortably back in his chair, hands crossed over an ample abdomen, and with a twinkle in his eye announced, "You are accepted." To my astonishment he added, "If it hadn't been for your father, I should never have gotten through City College." I could never figure out the meaning of that remark but wondered if some sort of peeking over shoulders had gone on, or the like.

Medical School

In any event, I turned up at Hopkins Medical School at the appointed time and there began a most miserable year as I recall it. Anatomy and the dissection of stiffs with the horrid odor of formaldehyde left me cold and repulsed, and even histology seemed beyond my grasp, though taught by Dr. Florence Sabin. Those dreary days were somewhat ameliorated by the kindness of A. Murray Fisher, a Baltimorean and Princeton classmate, who often invited several of us to spend weekends at the Fisher estate in the Greenspring Valley. Though we put in many hours of hard study over the weekends, Murray's mother treated us like young gods, and they were happy hours indeed. Mrs. Fisher was developing the first signs of Huntington's chorea, which ran in her family and was readily recognized by all of them. Sad to relate, Murray himself developed the disease and his death from it robbed Baltimore of one of its finest physicians, an expert in infectious diseases.

During that dreadful first year of medical school another happy incident occurred. Dr. Thomas R. Brown, Head of the Gastrointestinal Division of Medicine, to whose debutante daughter I paid some faint court, was a close friend of my father's. He invited me to dinner at Thanksgiving time, and after dinner over brandies he was kind enough to listen to my tale of woe. He cheered me no end by saying, "Think nothing of it. I hated the first year of medical school too. Wait until you get to MacCallum and Pathology and come to dinner next year at this time. If you then still want to get out of Medicine, I will do what I can to see that it is done with dignity and honor."

The sequel to this anecdote is that Dr. Brown did indeed remember and invited me again for dinner the next fall. By that time you could not have paid me to leave medical school. I could never discern what brought about this complete metamorphosis, for we were still dealing with dead material and spending hours on end looking through microscopes.

As a last recollection of that first year in medical school, my final examination in Anatomy comes to mind. It was an oral examination. Dr. Weed, the instructor, had graduated from Yale University and spent the first minutes discussing college athletics. He then reached into a wooden box and pulled out a small bone, flashed it in the air and caught it in his fist on the way down. "That was a wrist bone; which one was it?" he asked me, and I said I had no idea. "I don't either," he replied, and the conversation about Princeton and Yale football was resumed. The examination ended on that note. I was informed, I believe reliably, that my class standing at the end of that first year was next to lowest of those students retained. There was a custom then that a certain percentage of the first year class had to be dropped.

During the summer of 1925, after my first year in medical school, Dick Shackelford asked me to join him in chaperoning the first tourist third-class expedition to Europe aboard the Holland American line ship *Volendam*. The party was largely composed of college students of both sexes. They were mostly a well-behaved lot. Among them were the members of Sleepy Hall's jazz band on their way to a summer appointment at a nightclub in Paris. They played nightly for the third-class tourists, and because of their popularity many first-class passengers came down to our quarters at night. The first-class passengers reciprocated by inviting us on occasion to their luxurious quarters above. Shackelford's and my job was to keep order among the group, snooping about in lifeboats after dark to see that no mischief was afoot.

Among our group, as well as Hall's orchestra, were Benjamin Spock, a member of the Yale crew who would later become a world-famous pediatrician; Thomas McCann, later a partner in J. P. Morgan & Company; Tom Sargent, a Yale hockey player; and an instructor in English at Harvard College, Mr. Topping.

Musings and Reminiscences of a Pseudo-Scientist

Charles Garland, the captain of the Davis Cup tennis team, arranged for us to have tickets to Wimbledon and we saw the finals between Tilden and Patterson of Australia and also saw Garland and Richard Norris Williams win the doubles from a French pair.

After a brief stay in London, Sargent, McCann, Topping, Shackelford and I hired a car and toured through the lake country and Wales, stopping at pensions and eating mostly fish and chips. Interestingly enough the whole trip, including our stay in Paris, cost us no more than $250 apiece.

Dick Shackelford was anxious to fly from London to Paris. On the night before our scheduled flight we were dining in Soho when an extra edition of the evening papers appeared on the street. "French plane down in channel. All lost." Immediately I decided we should take the boat train, thus saving ourselves considerable money and perhaps our lives, but Shackelford insisted that the next flight would be the safest yet flown, and so the next morning we boarded a single-engine plane for Paris. Besides the pilot there was only one passenger along with Shackelford and myself, he being a very nonchalant Frenchman who immediately covered his face with a newspaper and went to sleep. We flew low over Deauville where bathers waved at us and then the pilot pointed to a black cloud which he thought he could beat to Paris. However, we collided with the cloud at Paris, and as we descended, lightning was flashing downward by our windows while flames from exhaust backfire were flashing upward. Though I have never had too much affinity for the French I was very happy to see the Gendarmes on the ground. It was some 50 years later that I was persuaded to get in another plane.

After some days in Paris we entrained for Bruges, Belgium using our American tourist guide book. We drove up to a pension at 10 P.M. to be greeted in unwelcome fashion, the pension being strictly for females. But a nearby hotel took us in and we spent two days exploring that lovely city. From there we went to Normandy and stayed a week at the quaint Isle de Brehat. There we breakfasted at the house of a dear old lady, eating her freshly baked bread from a brick oven and evenings netting the abundant shrimp which came in with the tide and cooking them over open fires on the beach. It was a glorious week.

We spent my birthday, August 27, 1925, riding the Seine River boat and consuming perhaps a bit too much French beer. The homeward journey on the *Volendam* was uneventful, though with many passengers different from those with whom we had crossed. Thus I entered the second year of medical school rejuvenated and with a wholly different perspective.

In that second year all turned to gold, and under McCallum's magic, the whole thing became a glorious game and fun. When the time came to see patients, under the guidance of such expert teachers as Drs. Louis Hamman, Samuel Wolman, John Dorsey, Charles Austrian, and Henry Thomas, life became even more exciting. My lack of astuteness became apparent when Dr. Longcope held his first session with us on physical diagnosis. Though he had held the post of Professor of Medicine and Department Chairman for several years, I did not recognize his face or name. He presented me with an adolescent white girl and asked me what I noticed. My reply was that she appeared to be Oriental but he gently replied, "No, her eyes look that way because they are swollen with water—she has acute nephritis."

The ward years were even more exciting. Each year a few of us were given the privilege of being substitute interns, whenever the regular holder of that position was on vacation. It was here that I think my greatest instruction in clinical medicine came. The house staff treated us as equals and went out of their way to teach us all they knew. It was at this point in time that an event took place that profoundly affected my subsequent career.

The Marbury family, who lived next door to us, was accustomed to having Sunday evening supper parties to which their children were permitted to invite guests. Sylvine Marbury had married Thomas Harrold, a gynecologic resident, and he invited two of his young companions on the medical service to supper. It was here that I had my first contact with Fuller Albright and Read Ellsworth. These two exciting young investigators took kindly to my questions and, as it were, "took me under their wing." I became their scut boy, performing all sorts of menial tasks under their strict discipline, but gained thereby exposure to all their thoughts and intriguing imaginations. They were interested, among other things, in the parathyroid glands and were the first to describe a case of idiopathic (unknown cause) hypoparathyroidism. The patient, an Italian adolescent, would have frequent attacks of tetany and would appear evenings in the accident room with severe carpo-pedal spasms and sometimes convulsions. He refused to obey orders not to take vigorous exercise and would play basketball of an evening, which served to induce the tetany. To stop the tetany and save his life, he urgently needed to have the blood concentration of calcium elevated. The only solution of calcium we then had which could be administered intravenously was calcium chloride which, though dramatically effective, was fraught with the dangers of corroding the tissues if even tiny amounts were delivered outside the vein. It was a harrowing existence and I was lucky to have avoided inducing tissue necrosis in the boy.

Ellsworth, a Johns Hopkins graduate, had gone to Massachusetts General Hospital as a house officer. Here he met Albright and persuaded him to apply to Hopkins for assistant residency under Longcope, Ellsworth meanwhile having returned to Johns Hopkins as Chief Resident. Thus, when he came to Baltimore, Albright resumed his close friendship with Ellsworth, whose brilliant mind, in my opinion, was very influential in promoting Albright's later successes.

In the middle of my fourth year as medical student, I was the happy recipient of an exchange student arrangement made between Dr. Longcope and Dr. Howard Means. I spent two months as house pupil at Massachusetts General Hospital, where I was taken under the kindly wing of Dr. Oliver Cope, then a fourth-year student at Harvard. It was through Bill Marbury, an old friend of Cope's, that I was provided with this happy introduction to Harvard. Cope became one of my closest friends, a relationship which has happily continued ever since. It was arranged that I live, while in Boston, at the Lancet Club, a wing of the newly built Vanderbilt Hall for medical students. We traversed the distance to MGH in John Edsall's ancient jalopy and one weekend Cope, Edsall and I drove to Concord, Mass., and spent a sort of holiday at the inn. Edsall's jalopy was open and we nearly froze to death going to Concord in a winter snowstorm.

I applied for internship at Massachusetts General, which then withheld appointments until late in March and required both oral and written examinations. That oral examination will remain forevermore in my memory. Seated at a long table with four elderly and very distinguished Boston physicians as interviewers, all glaring at me, the first question asked was "What would you do if you saw a man, a painter, in the accident room with bad abdominal pain of several day's duration, who had had no bowel movements for one week? He also had a black line on his gums." Having come into fairly close contact with Dr. Joseph Aub while at Massachusetts General Hospital, my immediate reply was that I would put him on a high calcium diet. A very stern committee member immediately asked, "If you were writhing in pain would you take kindly to eating a large bowl of spinach?" My second reply was I would give some morphine and atropine, whereupon the remainder of the interview took a more normal course.

Dr. Longcope had earlier denied my application for internship on his service, ostensibly because I was a Baltimorean, had matriculated at Princeton, and said it would be wise for me to go away for awhile to see how things were done elsewhere; and that if I performed creditably, he would consider putting me back on his house staff. But time was running out; nearly all my friends had received their appointments and here were all my apples in one basket.

The evening after the examinations at MGH were held, Mrs. Giles Thomas, wife of a Harvard fourth-year medical student and then secretary to Dr. Means, invited me to dinner before I left for New York to meet Lucy Iglehart, to whom I had recently become affianced. Noting my anxiety, Mrs. Thomas said, "I know I am breaking the rules, but I can't help breaking the rules to tell you that you and Myles Baker were chosen for the first two house officer appointments." My homeward journey was thus one of bliss.

I recall little of that fourth year back at Hopkins except frequent journeys to lunch with Lucy, who would pick me up at the Pithotomy Club and we would eat somewhere downtown. Our trips were often detected in restaurants with resulting jibes and allegations, since our engagement had not then been announced.

Musings and Reminiscences of a Pseudo-Scientist

At my bachelor dinner prior to our wedding, an interesting event took place, since widely quoted and oft incorrectly. The dinner was at the old Baltimore Club at Charles and Madison Streets, opposite an equestrian statue of my great-great-grandfather, John Eager Howard. After innumerable mint juleps made by Emmanuel Chambers, the Club's major-domo, who afterward occupied a similar position at the Maryland Club and became a close friend to many prominent Baltimoreans, the dinner finally ended. I was persuaded (foolishly, for I had just sprained an ankle playing in a tennis tournament) to be hoisted up on the statue and sit behind the likeness of my great-great-grandfather. Bruno Hills was the anchor man and C. D. Jackson next. It was terrifyingly high up there and when it came time to descend, I was having qualms. A burly policeman arrived on the scene and demanded to know, "Who do you think you are?" When told truthfully, he said, "Oh yeah, tell it to the judge." When persuaded of the truth, the policeman became the anchor man for my descent and all returned home most amicably.

Lucy and I were married June 30, 1928, at St. Thomas Church at Garrison Forest, and there followed what now seems to me a very sumptuous reception at Lucy's family's home in the Greenspring Valley. A brief wedding trip followed to the Virginia Hot Springs, where I won a tennis tournament which happened to be going on. The remainder of the summer was spent at the Iglehart home in the Valley or at their summer residence, a cottage on Upper Saranac Lake in the Adirondacks.

While at Saranac, we were invited on an evening picnic by George Packard. It was a cookout, and George had put kerosene for the fire into some of the beer bottles. These got mixed up and in the dark I was handed a bottle, presumably beer. The kerosene burned my throat but I vomited promptly and fortunately no harm was done. Drinking kerosene is not recommended, however.

Boston

Early in September we arrived as directed in Boston and moved into a small apartment at the corner of Charles and Revere Streets just at the foot of Beacon Hill. It was three blocks from MGH and I reported on time at the appointed date to be met by the Director, Dr. Washburn, a very imposing individual who was supposed to be very dictatorial.

The house staff hierarchy was strict and precise. One started at the foot of the ladder and was entitled "subskunk." The subskunk's duties were to appear at precisely 7:00 A.M. at the ward laboratory, where blood, urine and stool samples were placed to be analyzed. After finishing this chore and putting results on the ward charts, one's duties carried him to the outpatient clinic for skin and venereal diseases, where one drew buckets of blood for Wasserman reactions and the like, and did innumerable spinal taps on patients one never saw again. Afternoons were spent on the skin ward, fortunately under the direction of an expert nurse who knew more dermatology than most of the physicians. This was fortunate since the ward was filled with horrible exanthemata, and patients with exfoliative dermatitis for which we could do little except administer oatmeal baths. Miss Willard, the head nurse, looked kindly on my youth and inexperience and guided me in many ways. At MGH in those days prescriptions were handed out by numbers in a formulary (ointment 19, apply as directed) or digitalis would be ordered, tablets #75, take one twice daily. This applied even to orders written on the wards for inpatients.

My Harvard confreres on the house staff had been instructed to know just what to prescribe and do once the proper diagnosis had been achieved. In this regard I felt very inferior to them since we had been taught little or no therapeutics, of which indeed there existed very little worthwhile to the patient anyway.

The senior resident when I began on the West Medical Service was

Linn Fenimore Cooper, a delightful chap, full of humor and an excellent physician. His junior was Henry Fuller, a charming, diminutive individual from a town in Central Florida called Mulberry. He later returned home and became the recognized ablest internist in Central Florida.

The subsequent quarter was spent as "skunk," where one was but slightly higher on the hierarchy, but the duties were to be flunky to the pup. His duties in turn were to run all the routine administration of the wards, see that orders for x-rays were carried out, look at all x-rays with the visiting radiologist and have them on hand for viewing at ward rounds by the visiting physicians, and see that the paper work on charts was kept in order, as well as keeping the sub-skunk and skunk busy and thoroughly subjugated.

When the stage of junior and senior was reached the setting began getting tough and the responsibilities greatly increased. Alternate days admissions were sent either to the West or East service. Every other reception day the junior or senior would be held responsible for the patients admitted. It was he who chose which patients were presented to the visiting physician, Dr. William H. Smith ("Big Bill"), who visited much of my term as junior, and had to be met at the main entrance of the hospital at precisely 10:00 A.M. with a red rose. Dr. Smith was then escorted through the various corridors to the proper ward in the old Bullfinch Building, where in turn he was met by the head nurse with an immaculate white butcher's coat into which she pinned the rose.

The wards were set up with the head nurse's desk in the center of a huge room, the patients' beds being aligned close to the walls, separated only by their curtains, not drawn most of the time. Rounds would be conducted with chairs in a circle around the nurse's desk; the student would present the history upon which great emphasis was laid, sadly not always true today. After some discussion among students and house staff, the "professor" would be led to the bedside to examine the patient. Further discussions then followed, a tentative diagnosis devised and diagnostic studies and a therapeutic program arranged.

Promptly at 11:00 A.M. a junior nurse arrived with a cup of tomato soup with crackers and a thin slice of onion. Dr. Smith would pass the onion gently through the soup and while standing and discussing the case would sip the soup. I never heard it authentically stated, but all this was presumably because Dr. Smith suffered from a peptic ulcer. Another case would then be presented, whereupon Dr. Smith would be escorted by the senior or junior and most of the rest of the retinue to the hospital's main entrance. The whole thing took on the nature of a melodrama, but strict discipline was observed and the results proved the method highly successful in training future physicians.

There were several diverting incidents in my immediate recall. Much fanfare was created when a young, delirious typhoid patient got out of his bed and was found defecating on the head nurse's desk shouting, "Hey mom! Come pull the chain!"

There was an annual celebration held in which former house officers gathered and for whom what would now be called a "Grand Rounds" was held. A house officer would present a case for discussion. On one of those occasions celebrities such as Doctors Robert Loeb, Isaac Starr, George Minot and others were present when the house officer presented a dear old lady with sepsis. He asked her if she had chills, which seemed to mean nothing to her, and trying to be helpful I asked, "Did your teeth chatter?" With a charming smile, she replied " 'Deed not, they wasn't in," which brought down the house.

It often seemed to me that we house officers were given too much responsibility for the stage of our maturity and wisdom. Though I recall no nervous breakdowns during my term of service, as juniors and seniors we had no recourse to more expert advice. It was unheard of to call the visiting physician and ask for help. There were so-called residents—now they would be called Fellows—attached to the senior staff members such as Dr. Means, Arley Bock, Joseph Aub, and Walter Bauer, but these men were usually even less experienced in clinical medicine than we were. One's best recourse was to ask his opposite on the other medical service for help. I recall vividly an experience one night in the accident ward to which I had been called in emergency consultation. A girl of 14 had had a sore throat for several days and developed abdominal pain. A surgical intern thought he could hear a friction at the right costal margin, which

Musings and Reminiscences of a Pseudo-Scientist   19

I could not. The temperature was only 100°, white count 10,000, but I became convinced that she had appendicitis. My opposite number on the Surgical Service was called in consultation. The surgical house staff could not operate on emergencies without calling the visiting surgeon, who was obliged to come. Dr. Cope called a disgruntled surgeon, whose name I think was Miller, who confronted me with "Young man, if your diagnosis is correct you have saved a child; if not, you have killed a child." But he operated and I sat high in the ether dome looking down on the procedure. Dr. Cope says I was pale as death but, when the peritoneal cavity was opened and there was exposed a red hot appendix, the color flushed back to my face. In those days a general anesthetic given to a patient with pneumonia usually resulted in death.

Another incident with a less happy ending occurred in the emergency ward, but will live forever in my memory and was most instructive. Dr. Myles Baker, my counterpart on the East medical service, called me to assist in the care of a young girl in diabetic coma. Under administration of intravenous sodium chloride and insulin, things seemed to be coming along smoothly, blood sugar falling nicely and ketonuria falling. Suddenly there was gurgling in the throat and the child went into pulmonary edema. At postmortem the mitral valve was found tightly closed, a fact none of us had realized, there being no audible murmurs, and we were given no history of previous heart trouble. But the episode paid dividends.

Several years later at Johns Hopkins, when Dr. James Bordley and I were seeing all the cases of diabetic coma, we decided to have a three-way stop-cock on all the intravenous rigs and this permitted us to monitor frequently the venous pressure, which is usually very low; and at the first evidence of an abrupt rise, the intravenous drip would be slowed. In those days the therapy of diabetic coma was not always successful, and our pathologists told us they found no pathologic cause of death, but, clinically, the patient seemed for all the world to have died of "shock," as after excessive hemorrhage. The three-way stop-cock also permitted us to take frequent measurements of the hematocrit, and if this did not fall it simply indicated that our intravenous fluid was running out of the capillaries as fast as we were putting it in; thus we were failing to increase the markedly restricted blood volume. Just such an event happened one evening when Dr. Bordley and I were treating a young man in deep coma. We decided that we must put something besides salt solution into the blood system, something which would not leak out of the capillaries and would expand the blood volume. To our gratification the young man responded to the transfusion therapy and recovered. In those days, the fairly young insulin days, the elder physicians who had seen much coma before the use of insulin would assess at the bedside just how long the patient would live. Doctors Longcope, Harrop and Carter had seen the boy and predicted only a few hours of life. When they saw the patient the next morning, quite chipper, their astonishment was great. Ever since, I have used the three-way stop-cock to make frequent checks on the hematocrit and venous pressure, but find the method seldom used nowadays and have been unable to persuade our house officers of its value and to use it routinely.

For exercise, of which we got really plenty racing the hospital corridors, Myles Baker, the national squash champion, decided to teach me the game and we joined the Union Boat Club, a few steps from MGH, and periodically played squash on their semi-open courts in very icy weather indeed. Baker was a very strenuous instructor and the game generally ended 21 to 0 in his favor. In those days one had to win a point to get service, and only the server could win a point that counted. Occasionally there would be tennis matches with house staff of other hospitals, which always seemed to come out with the Brigham or City house staffs on the short end.

At Myles Baker's wedding I was happy to be asked to be an usher. What I remember best about the wedding was the toast Myles's father gave to the bride and groom: "Welcome to that wonderful state of matrimony, in which all joys are doubled, all sorrows halved." The elder Dr. Baker was Professor of Dramatics and Fine Arts at Yale.

Those were exciting days in medicine, when things were developing such that one could really begin to help patients. Pernicious anemia was under heavy study and Dr. William Castle, a former MGH house officer, would come over from City Hospital with normal gastric juice which we would incubate overnight with beef and then introduce it into the stomach of a patient with pernicious anemia the following morning. The effects on blood response were dramatic. I can recall an instance, however, when Dr. Means strictly censured Castle and me for applying the test to a patient with very profound anemia, who Dr. Means felt was in imminent danger of death and should have been transfused. However, the patient responded beautifully and no harm had come from the experiment.

In the spring of 1929, our eldest son was born, prematurely and in the middle of the night. The professor of obstetrics, a German Geheimrat if ever there was one, seemed indignant to be inconvenienced by a young house officer's wife and gave me short shrift during my wait in the obstetrics quarters. Before leaving he informed me that my son's chances of survival were poor, but with the greatest care and kindness, a young pediatrician recommended by Dr. Means brought him through completely whole.

Early Hopkins Postgraduate Years

My term of appointment ended June 30, 1930, and it became important to give thought to succeeding years. Dr. Means kindly offered me a new job being created as Chief Resident to the Philips House, the private pavilion of the MGH, but our roots were in Baltimore, and both Lucy and I yearned to return there.

I applied for an assistant residency in the Marburg Pavilion of the Johns Hopkins, then supervised by Dr. Llewellys Barker. This was considered a less desirable post than one on Dr. Longcope's Osler Service, the competition being thus less keen, and both Murray Fisher, who had been at Presbyterian Hospital in New York while I had been in Boston, and I were promptly accepted. I got the impression that Dr. Longcope was somewhat ruffled by our application to the private service. Both Fisher and I were strongly attracted by the excellent practicing physicians then staffing the Marburg. These included Doctors Barker, William Sidney Thayer, Charles Austrian, Thomas Boggs, Walter Baetjer, Sidney Miller, and many others—all superb clinicians. These men took us in as partners, allowing many responsibilities for their patients and making every effort to teach us their skills. I have never regretted the year on Marburg and believe my clinical skills were greatly enhanced there.

While assistant resident in Marburg, Dr. Samuel Crowe, for whom it was my privilege in later years to be personal physician, did radical antral operations on my nose. I had had much trouble during medical school and it was finally decided to operate. There had been sinus trouble also while I was house officer at Massachusetts General and I can remember with horror spending ten days in our apartment with daily visits from Dr. William H. Smith who religiously sought for petechiae, felt for my spleen and listened to my heart, all because of a low-grade fever and stuffy nose. His specialty was bacterial endocarditis and, though he didn't mention to me what he was after, it was perfectly obvious and scared the daylights out of me.

While recuperating from Dr. Crowe's operation, a heart-warming incident occurred which doubtless would not be repeated today. Dr. Winford Smith, Director of the hospital, visited my rooms and said "Don't worry about the bills" (it was in the midst of the Great Depression and everyone was broke); "we at Hopkins take care of our own."

After the operative period it was decided I needed two weeks in the sun, and through the good graces of Dr. Ralph Hills, I became acquainted with the Hillsboro Club in Pompano Beach, Florida. Lucy and I returned there many subsequent years. Prior to a visit during the height of the war, Dr. Bowman, President of the Johns Hopkins University, phoned to ask if while in Florida I would be willing to see Winston Churchill. The then-Ambassador to London, a friend of Bowman's, had phoned him to see if a Hopkins doctor could see Churchill, who had been persuaded to take a much-needed rest in Florida and about whose health he had become alarmed. For two weeks at Hillsboro I waited anxiously for a phone call from Churchill which never came. After embarking on a battleship bound for Miami, the Prime Minister had suddenly recuperated and would have no part of seeing any doctors. But on another occasion, I had a chance to view Mr. Churchill, if not meet him. There was a big conference going on at the home of Mr. Stettinius, which was just two houses north along the Hillsboro beach. Dr. Hills and I once casually strolled up the beach observing from a distance a large rotund individual puffing a long cigar and talking animatedly with two other men, who turned out to be Lord Beaverbrook and Stettinius. Out of the bushes there suddenly appeared three huge young men, obviously Secret Service guards, who courteously told us they knew we meant no harm but please to come no further. We beat a hasty retreat.

There were many memorable events during the Marburg year. We saw the first case of drug toxicity, I believe, unfortunately in the sister of one of our physicians. The hepatitis, which proved fatal, was believed by Dr. Louis Hamburger to be due to the taking of cincophen for joint trouble. The case alerted others to further possibilities. Soon other cases were reported and the drug was removed from the market.

There, too, I saw my first patient with agranulocytosis. She was the wife of the President of the American Bar Association, a patient of Dr. Sidney Thayer's from Memphis. Dr. Thayer had left her in my care while he was away briefly, with instructions to call in any of his confreres if anything went wrong. One morning on rounds I entered her room to be greeted with, "My white blood count is going down." She had experienced an episode of agranulocytosis before, and described vividly the sensation as if all strength was being sapped from her. Her temperature was normal but by the time Dr. Crowe, Chief of Otolaryngology, arrived, it had risen sharply and her throat was covered with white exude. I don't recall the drug she had been taking, but it was immediately stopped. She recovered and to my knowledge had no more attacks of the disorder.

I was witness to one of Dr. Louis Hamman's superb diagnoses. A man known to have an arterio-venous aneurysm in his thigh over which there was a loud bruit was in the hospital with fever of unknown origin. Dr. Hamman concluded that his disorder so resembled bacterial endocarditis that he must be suffering a similar disorder, the organism being attached to the inner lining of his aneurysm instead of to a heart valve. Dr. Rienhoff removed the aneurysm where the situation was found to be exactly as Dr. Hamman predicted and the patient made an immediate recovery.

One evening Dr. Barker received an emergency call to have a patient admitted from Lancaster, Pennsylvania. He asked me to see the patient on arrival and report back to him. It was clear that the man was suffering from a large left pleural effusion, and I so reported. The patient received immediate relief when the chest was tapped but in my enthusiasm I kept removing the fluid until a volume of 4 liters was reached. The next morning Dr. Barker pointed out rather strictly that I might have induced "mediastinal flutter" from removing so much fluid so quickly, a lesson I never forgot. Unfortunately the effusion was due to an hypernephroma, which had invaded the thoracic cavity and the poor fellow never recovered.

Another experience for which I was not given a 4-plus grading was shared with Dr. Murray Fisher. An elderly man suffering with hypertension suddenly became afflicted with severe bronchospasm. To all the world it was an attack of bad asthma. Dr. Fisher and I administered adrenalin (epinephrine) to the patient with dramatic recovery, but the next day the patient's physician was not enthusiastic about our performance. To this day I haven't understood how the adrenalin proved so effective, if indeed "cardiac asthma" was the correct diagnosis.

The Osler Service Years: (1930-1932)

Read Ellsworth was still in Baltimore and my interest in investigative medicine was rekindled. I thus applied the following year for an assistant residency on the Osler Service and Dr. Longcope kindly accepted me. It was through Ellsworth's influence that I stayed on later in the Division of Endocrinology and Metabolism as a Fellow for two years under the direct supervision of Dr. George Harrop, but most closely associated with Ellsworth.

On our return to Baltimore, Lucy and I rented a small house on dingy Wolfe Street across from the hospital. Though the quarters were primitive and limited we were in good company. For in the same block lived the Myles Bakers, whom I had persuaded to take a year or two with Longcope; the George Finneys, the Eldridge Campbells, Mrs. Campbell having been Eleanor Brown, as previously mentioned in these recollections. Also there were the Townley Patons, he later to become a distinguished ophthalmologist in New York and the Arab countries, and the Austin Lamonts, later to become Head of the Anesthesia Department. Our neighbors were thus a distinguished and most congenial lot, though social activities among us were kept at a minimum.

Among my compatriots on the Osler Medical Service were Dr. Richard Beebe, a Princeton and Hopkins Medical School graduate, afterward to become Chairman of the Medical Department at Albany; Dr. Caroline Bedell (later Thomas), who became a world-renowned cardiologist; Dr. Warde B. Allan of Montreal, later to become my brother-in-law by marrying Lucy's sister, and a popular Baltimore internist and teacher in the medical school.

Each assistant resident had his turn in the accident room and, when admitting a patient to another man's floor, was not averse to "laying him an egg." On one occasion I saw a black man with a fever of 108° and seemingly moribund. My note on the record (it was a hot summer night) said simply "typical siriasis." Dr. Murray Fisher, no Latin scholar, had a hard time figuring out the meaning but finally found the definition in the dictionary and successfully administered the appropriate therapy for sunstroke.

Theoretically, the assistant residents were "off" every other evening, but it didn't happen very often if the ward load was heavy. But if indeed one could finish up by five o'clock, he escorted his substitute on rounds, explaining all the patients, but we could be sure that substitute had combed every patient for possible missed diagnoses, which would be pointed out with much glee the next morning. But there was little malice among the group, and in retrospect we really had a glorious time.

Grand rounds were held one morning each week, when the entire staff, including visiting physicians, would attend while one or two patients were presented to Dr. Longcope. On one such occasion on our ward, when Dr. Harrop was attending, both Dr. Carter and Dr. Longcope heard a diastolic murmur that had escaped the rest of us. I don't recall whether or not the murmur had any clinical significance, but Dr. Harrop seemed always to feel himself demeaned as a clinician by Longcope and said to me afterwards that "If there is a diastolic murmur there, you can use my head for a football." There was more feeling of competitive rivalry, even jealousy then, among the upper staff than among us juniors, especially between full- and part-time staff members. It must be recalled that this was quite early in the days of full-time staff having been begun at Hopkins, a pretty tumultuous time and a subject where tempers sometimes flared. There was no question but that as clinicians, the part-time men were a vastly superior lot, with the exception of Dr. Longcope, who was a master clinician and bedside teacher.

When my two years on the Osler Service had run out, I was appointed as "Fellow in Medicine" attached to the division then known as chemical but in fact was devoted to endocrinology and metabolism. My salary was the largest then received by a Fellow at Hopkins, $1,800 per annum.

Though having some activities in the caring for Dr. Harrop's and Dr. Ellsworth's patients, I was really more of a laboratory technologist, one of my duties being to run all the serum calcium determinations for the hospital. It was in the early days of parathyroid excitement and I ran innumerable calciums for physicians groping for an answer which, under the circumstances, I was in no position to refuse, though nearly all results were normal. Dr. Harrop's major interest at that time was in adrenal insufficiency (Addison's disease) and there was much dog experimental work going on in his laboratory with salt replacement in an effort to protect adrenalectomized dogs. Dr. Harrop had also contacted the Professors of Physiology at Princeton, Doctors Pfifner and Swingle, seeking some adrenal extract which avowedly saved the lives of smaller animals that had been adrenalectomized. Dr. Leonard Rowntree, formerly of Hopkins but then at the Mayo Clinic, gave a group of reporters an interview in which he bewailed the issuance to Baltimore of the Princeton extract, since the Mayo Clinic had so many more patients with Addison's disease than did Johns Hopkins. The interview was published in the *New York Times* which infuriated Dr. Harrop, who received less of the adrenal extract from Princeton because of the force of public pressure. The whole thing was pretty much a tempest in a teapot because it did require several hundred cc's of the scarce extract to have any influence at all on a patient ill with adrenal insufficiency. One of Dr. Harrop's patients with Addison's disease developed abdominal pain on a Saturday afternoon. I called Dr. Dean Lewis, the Chairman of the Department of Surgery, to see the boy. He agreed with the diagnosis of appendicitis but wanted to know if I wished him to kill the boy or let nature do it, for in those days almost any traumatic experience was enough to cause death in an Addisonian, but Dr. Lewis operated and as he predicted, the patient died soon thereafter.

A patient appeared on Marburg with every indication of Addison's disease but with normal blood pressure. This was very puzzling until it was learned that for several years, he had been treated for high blood pressure. The appearance of the adrenal insufficiency had given him hypotension relative to the blood pressure to which he was accustomed. Something to remember.

When parathyroid hormone became available, Ellsworth devised his test, which also bears my name, for determining the response to the hormone by measuring the changes in urinary phosphorus after injection of the hormone. My part in these studies was to prepare the material for intravenous injection, administer it and make determinations on the blood and urine calcium and phosphorus. It was nasty looking stuff, more like scum off a spring pond than anything else, but though I gave innumerable injections of it, to my recollection there were no adverse reactions. Patients whose parathyroids had inadvertantly been removed during thyroid surgery (and we had not a few of them) responded to the test with sharp increases in their urinary phosphorus. Those with so-called pseudohypoparathyroidism (Fuller Albright's Seabright Bantam syndrome) did not.

It was during those fellowship years that I began to have close contact with the Department of Urology and Dr. Hugh Young. Young was very fond of Ellsworth and asked him to see many of the extraordinary number of patients that flocked to his door. Among these were individuals who displayed all sorts of urologic abnormalities, especially those with sexual aberrations. Several of these patients remain vividly in my memory. There was a young male in whom Dr. Young found on cystoscopy a connection between urethra which was hypospadic and an internal cavity containing a minuscule uterus. The patient was short, muscular, with abundant beard and a deep voice. He had had an early adolescence and been raised as a male. His desire was to be married and arrangements had been made but, being a Catholic, he had consulted a priest who denied permission unless Dr. Young pronounced him a male. While Dr. Young was debating the matter, the young man arrived dead in the accident ward, having committed suicide. This was, of course, one of the early cases we began seeing with congenital adrenal hyperplasia, in which years later, in the late 1940s when cortisone became available, Dr. Lawson Wilkins's intuitive reasoning made possible correction of the disorder and permitted these persons to become normal functioning females except for certain irreversible anatomic problems including deep voices and heavy beards.

Soon thereafter Dr. Young operated on two Canadian sisters with this disorder, carrying out subtotal adrenalectomy, on the ground that if subtotal thyroidectomy cured hyperthyroidism, why would not subtotal adrenalectomy overcome the endocrine abnormalities in this disorder? Both patients went through the most horrendous postoperative courses, with high fevers and shock, but survived, though exhibiting no improvement in the course of their disorders since their remaining adrenal tissue simply continued to hypertrophy under the stimulus of adrenocorticotropic hormone. It was through these associations with Dr. Young that Dr. Samuel Vest and I a few years later became interested in the clinical use of male sex hormones, a bizarre tale which I shall relate anon.

While Dr. Vest and I were doing our first experimental testing of testosterone and found it to be a potent stimulator of male sex drive, Dr. Hugh Young, ever alert for a bit of publicity, told some newspaper reporters that we were about to report some interesting news at a medical society meeting. He persuaded us to talk with the reporters, which we agreed to do provided there would be no dramatizing in their reports. The reporters kept their word but the headline writer did not and the papers had screaming headlines "Hopkins Doctors find Fountain of Youth." I was so inundated with phone calls that I sought refuge for a week in Dr. Baetjer's home until the excitement had died down. Moral: Don't trust the press unless you have headline writers included in the promise.

But it was about this time that Read Ellsworth died, stricken suddenly with tuberculous pneumonia, uniformly fatal at that time. Ellsworth's death was a great loss to the Hopkins medical fraternity and deprived the world of one of its most exciting and brilliant clinical investigators.

War Years

The war years were hectic times at Hopkins, as with all other medical institutions. I had signed up with the Johns Hopkins Medical Unit and we were due to go overseas within a few days. One evening I was phoned by some Washington official and told that my name had been removed from the unit and I was ordered to report at 9:00 A.M. two days hence at the office of Dr. Means in the Massachusetts General Hospital. No reasons were given.

It seems that the Army had predicted very heavy casualties, especially fractures, and that a committee was to be set up for the studies of trauma. Among others present that morning in Dr. Means's office were Fuller Albright, Allan Kenyon of Chicago, John Browne of Montreal, and several others later to become members of the Rochester, New York branch of the Atomic Energy Commission. Our group at Hopkins was to study especially methods to shorten the recovery time from fractures and prevention of kidney stones which were prominent sources of trouble with long-term immobilization. We set about our task quickly with the monies provided by the Office of Scientific Research and Development (OSRD). All the fracture patients who gave their permission and who had fractures requiring immobilization of large areas of the body were to be treated and studied on the research unit in cooperation with the Department of Orthopedic Surgery. My first idea conceived from the observation of Dr. Morton, a Rochester, New York surgeon, was to apply tourniquets above a fracture site to increase venous pressure in the part. The Rochester surgeon showed that such maneuvers had hastened healing of the fracture considerably in dogs. Dr. George Bennett, Orthopedic Chief, quickly quashed the idea on the ground that we would inevitably produce a rash of Volkmann's contractures, almost certainly correct. We became interested in the observations of Dr. Cuthbertson of Scotland that trauma of almost any kind produced an extraordinary waste of body protein with excessive nitrogen excretion in the urine. Cuthbertson's observations in experimental animals were observed to hold true for man also, and we spent much time and effort in attempts to block the huge nitrogen losses—all to no avail, for the subjects simply returned the added oral protein in the urine gram for gram. The nutritional losses from trauma were equivalent to those of total starvation as we observed in conscientious objectors who were assigned to us by the government for nutritional studies. They were the nicest group of boys imaginable, willingly undergoing all sorts of tests and dietary maneuvering.

It was during these studies on nutrition that we began using total intravenous feeding, a procedure which had been begun by a St. Louis surgeon. We used a caseine hydrolysate furnished us by Mead-Johnson Company, combined with sugar and water, with extraordinary success. At about this time Dr. Blalock received a physician patient from Cowpens, South Carolina, who had had a long-standing draining abscess from a ruptured appendix.*

---

*It is of some interest that I met this physician again when we went to Cowpens for the U.S. Bicentennial in 1976, for here my great-great-grandfather distinguished himself, the first to rout Tarleton's British Regulars. He is said to have disobeyed orders at the battle; having been ordered to retreat, instead he ordered a "charge." When confronted with possible court-martial, he is said to have replied, "Had I not been successful, I wouldn't be here to be court-martialed."

We were asked to give total intravenous feeding to this emaciated individual and when Dr. Blalock operated some days later, he was amazed to find the gut limp and empty, making the operation much simpler than any similar procedure he had ever done. There was no postoperative distension either, and we successfully used this procedure on several subsequent patients, to the surgeons' complete satisfaction.

All these things were reported both at the so-called Macy Meetings and the OSRD Meetings, both of which took place at periodic times. At one such meeting in Washington I reported that a given amount of nitrogen by the intravenous method was handled by the body economy exactly as would be equivalent amounts fed as beef and potatoes. Dr. Isadore Ravdin practically called me a liar, for he said Jonathan Rhoads, on his service in Philadelphia, had tried the same thing and found that he could not maintain nitrogen balance with intravenous feeding. Years later, Dr. Ravdin publicly apologized for his words. By that time it had been found that the difference between Rhoads's experiments and ours had been that we had added potassium to our milk hydrolysate and he had not. Just why I added the potassium I cannot say, but I like to think that it was from Biblical knowledge that the Israelites were unable to make bricks without straw which led me to the conclusion that cells needed all their constituents in the environment to be able to rebuild themselves.

As an offshoot of all this, Dr. Elliot Newman and I noted that the induction of heart failure was associated with large protein breakdown and potassium loss. An experiment was carried out—I suspect without Dr. Longcope's knowledge—in which a well-compensated patient with mitral stenosis was evaluated a) when digitalis was withdrawn and he went into heart failure, and b) during recovery when digitalis was once more administered. This material was never published, and I have not seen the phenomenon quoted.

Macy Meetings Under the Auspices of OSRD

The so-called Macy Meetings held throughout the war and afterward were good fun. In the elegant surroundings of a New York apartment hotel, there would assemble a most interesting group, really led by Fuller Albright and Fremont-Smith, representing the Macy Foundation. Ephraim Shorr and Donald Whedon from Cornell, Robinson at first from Rochester, New York, Richard Follis and myself from Baltimore, William Neuman and Samuel Bassett from Rochester, Edward Reifenstein from Boston, and from time to time with guests from the United States and abroad, even marine physiologists and geologists, might be invited. The discussions were lively, usually on some predetermined subject, and various members were invited to report on their recent work. All this was done in an informal atmosphere and among luxurious surroundings, good food and drink. The idea that many circumstances resulted in the body's depletion of potassium was first reported here and as a direct result of our report that persons emerging from diabetic coma would accept enormous quantities of potassium, the first patient given potassium for hypokalemia in the treatment of diabetic acidosis was reported by Bassett of Rochester.

The first patient in diabetic acidosis to whom we had administered potassium intravenously was a pregnant woman seen in the obstetrical wards. Because I had no idea how much potassium to give or what strength to use, we asked the resident in Cardiology to come along and hitch her up to an electrocardiograph. About one-half hour after the infusion was begun, the cardiologist let out a whoop and said that the T wave was going off the map. The mixture was stopped and all was soon restored to normal, but the quantities of retained potassium proved to be astonishing.

A patient of Dr. William Grose was admitted to the hospital with a draining duodenal fistula. Despite enormous doses of intravenous sodium chloride, normally an acidifying agent, the serum bicarbonate kept rising. The salt was slowed and potassium added. Despite transient lowering of bicarbonate at the end of the day, by the next morning it would be back at its previous level until by the sixth day, when enormous quantities of potassium had been retained, it was normal and remained so. By this time we had access to a flame photometer which rendered rapid the quantitation of potassium in serum, whereas previously it had required days for the return of a chemical determination. The Lederle Company had designed and made the first flame photometer. They offered one to Dr. Peters at Yale, who promptly put it to good use. When the Joslin Clinic failed to accept one of the machines, it was offered to us. Harry Eisenberg, long-time expert technician for Dr. Harrop, and I journeyed to Peters's laboratory to learn how to run the machine. We were most graciously treated by Miss Pauline Hald, Dr. Peters's technician, and returned to Baltimore to set up shop. During the following summer, Dr. Daniel Darrow came to Baltimore to study summer diarrhea in children, a disease rare in New Haven and plentiful in Baltimore. From clinical astuteness, Darrow suspected hypokalemia in his infants and was grateful for our help in telling him what his infant patient's serum potassium was in a matter of minutes. Nowadays practically every administration of intravenous fluids contains potassium.

The Privilege of Caring for Dr. Edwards A. Park

A more delightful, knowledgeable, warm man, with boundless memory and a wry sense of humor, has probably never lived than Dr. Edwards A. Park, Chief of Pediatrics at Hopkins for many years. Dr. Finney remarked of him: "You could tell the warmth of the man as you shook his hand." To my amazement, I was called one morning by Dr. Park's long-time secretary, Miss Richards, to come to his office, for he was very ill. Dr. Park was found on the floor of his office, pale and dripping with perspiration and violently retching. This was the first of his many attacks of Meniere's disease, not very difficult to diagnose, but I had to let him lie right there until the dizziness passed. When asked how I happened to be called, Miss Richards replied that Dr. Park had so requested, saying that I was his personal physician.

During the summer of 1942, Dr. Park invited me and my two sons, ages about 14 and 12 years, to accompany him to his cabin on the Margaree River in Cape Breton, Nova Scotia. We caught a train to Boston and then boarded the "Gull" for the night ride to St. John, New Brunswick. It was crowded with soldiers, dirty, and arrived too late for us to make connection with our train to Cape Breton. We boarded the next train, a local, which went only as far as Monckton, New Brunswick, where we spent the night in leather armchairs in a ramshackle hotel across the street from the station. After writing some letters we wandered back to the railroad station. Seeking to mail our letters, we asked an attendant for the mailbox and were pointed to a door at the end of the passage. On arrival we were met by the sign "Men." On returning to the attendant displaying our letters, he replied, "Why didn't you say you wanted the post box?" We then boarded the train and were carried overnight to Orangedale on Cape Breton, where we arrived at 5:00 A.M. and were met for the forty-mile drive to Margaree.

We soon settled into the life of the cabin, the boys sleeping in a tent erected on a wooden platform. There were no plumbing facilities and we bathed (occasionally) in the cold waters of the Margaree and used the facilities of an outhouse for other purposes, but the cabin was warm and cozy, the food purchased locally by walking a mile was good, and we had no complaints about the milk purchased from the farmer who owned the land whereon the cabin rested. Dr. Park was not much of a cook, and the boys and I did most of the cooking. Salmon we had when we caught one—a rarity. Early in the morning we would repair to an adjacent pasture where,

Musings and Reminiscences of a Pseudo-Scientist

in a few moments, a basket of mushrooms could be gathered—delicious when fried right out of the field. Dr. Park was most kind and patient in teaching us the art of salmon fishing, ignoramuses that we were. Dr. Park tied his own flies and was generous in their distribution. Some evenings the only doctor within thirty miles would come over to the cabin, asking advice about his patients and often bringing some of them along. This was great fun, as Dr. Park was the god of the island. When he would come to a salmon pool with someone already fishing and others waiting, we would always be invited to fish first, since we were with Dr. Park.

Since then we have made many return visits to Margaree, always with the greatest pleasure. The people of the valley, mostly Scottish and Irish with a smattering of French, are most friendly and hospitable. With some help from Dr. Helen Taussig and ourselves, a toilet and power have since been added to the cabin, a gas stove installed instead of the kerosene burners we had first used, and an oil furnace installed, to help keep the chill off the sometimes chilly nights, even in August.

An interesting tale is told (not apocryphal) of Dr. Park once going to Margaree in a station wagon accompanied by a friend. Mrs. Park had loaded the station wagon and was to follow by air at a later date. When they reached the Canadian border the officer, seeking contraband, closely inspected the contents of the station wagon. To Dr. Park's utter astonishment, two cases of whiskey were discovered. Mrs. Park, who rather loved a nip now and then, had surreptitiously loaded the whiskey in with the other goods to take care of her wants over the summer. The officer correctly discerned that Dr. Park was no hardened rum runner and kept the whiskey at the border with a promise of its return on the homeward journey, a promise that was kept.

Dr. Park literally suffered the tortures of the damned from recurrent bouts of tic doloreux, an episodic disorder of unknown cause. During attacks, even the softest stroking of the face or gums created excruciating stabs of pain during which tears came to his eyes and he held his hands before his face. These were accepted stoically and fortunately, with advancing age, they recurred at longer and longer intervals.

In his eighties, Dr. Park tired more and more easily. He always ran a bradycardia and mild hypotension, but had no symptoms of heart failure. I was woefully slow in suspecting auricular fibrillation and heart block, but when it was discovered a pacemaker was inserted most successfully.

At his death on his beloved Margaree at age 90, I was visiting at the Margaree but not staying in the Park cabin, but Helen Taussig was there. I was summoned hastily by Helen to come at once, that Dr. Park had suffered a heart attack. There was nothing to do but administer opiates, which was done, and stand by to watch developments with tender care. About four days later Dr. Park began to cough up blood-tinged sputum and showed rales at one lung base. In retrospect, he had probably suffered a pulmonary embolus, but since there was also some fever we drove the thirty miles to the nearest drugstore and obtained some penicillin. But he died peacefully in his sleep a few days later. He was buried in a cemetery lot belonging to the Ross family, on whose property the cabin was built.

There is a curious story still current among Margaree inhabitants, that when the undertakers arrived to care for the body they were startled to hear a clicking noise from the chest. The story goes that it was the cardiac pacemaker still operating.

I had been forced to leave Margaree before Dr. Park's death by a promise to the Oliver Copes to come to Boston to see Dr. Cope professionally. As we were driving from Maine to Cape Breton, after a cruise with Cope and others, our car was stopped at the border by a customs guard standing in the middle of the road. We were startled because one entering Canada is not even noticed on the U.S. side, and further startled by instructions to call the sheriff of Machias at once. From him we learned that Dr. Cope had suffered a recurrence of urinary bleeding, which had commenced on the cruise we had taken together the week before but of which he had not informed me. Knowing that we were driving to Margaree, Dr. Cope's secretary called the sheriff asking that we be stopped; but by that time we had passed Machias so the message was relayed to the Canadian border.

The Post-War Years

There can be few happier times had than to have a group of young, enthusiastic, highly intelligent and friendly physicians come together to carry out clinical investigation. Beginning with Samuel Asper's return to Baltimore, William C. Thomas from Florida, Thomas Connor of Baltimore, Edmund Yendt from Toronto, Gemmell Morgan from Scotland, Richard Myers from Washington, Robert Mason of Baltimore, and Lillian Haddock, at present Dean at the University of Puerto Rico's Medical School and Editor of the new *Puerto Rico Health Sciences Journal*, just such a group came together at Hopkins in Endocrinology and Metabolism. Many of these doctors were referred by old friends and often were paid by the medical school to which they were scheduled to return. We were superbly assisted by Dr. Charles Bills who, after retirement from Mead Johnson & Company, had returned to Baltimore and volunteered his time and great skills to assist us. It was Dr. Bills who made a small fortune for Mead Johnson by the discovery of percomorph oil, and was a worldwide authority on vitamin D and its bioassay, having worked with Doctors McCollum and Abel prior to going to Indianapolis. Dr. Bills soon taught the group the techniques for determining the content of vitamin D by bioassasy. Using this technique, the group discovered that vitamin D (or at least its bioactive offspring) is carried almost entirely in the serum bound to an alphaglobulin.

The story of our involvement in renal ischemia and hypertension: serendipity, which is the accidental discovery of something other than what one is seeking, and luck both play major roles in clinical investigation.

At the suggestion of Dr. Maurice Pincoffs, Dr. Halsey Barker and I surveyed the world's literature in an attempt to identify a clinical picture of pheochromocytoma, which would be identifiable at the bedside. Because of this effort, we were asked by Dr. Holmes Boyd to see a patient who had been referred to him from Alabama. The patient's story was that he had been afflicted suddenly with right-sided abdominal pain and his abdomen had been explored seeking appendicitis, with negative findings. Soon after operation, it was found that he had developed acute hypertension. He was referred to Baltimore, where pheochromocytoma was suspected, because an injection of air around the kidneys was supposed to show a mass above the right kidney. Simultaneous explorations of the renal areas were made by Dr. Lloyd Lewis and Dr. Hugh Young. The tumor proved to be mythical, but during the operation the retractor of a young intern holding the right kidney slipped, bringing into view a yellowish mass in the kidney. Believing this mass to be malignant, Dr. Young removed the kidney. To everyone's amazement, the pathologists reported the mass to be an infarct (damaged tissue from an impeded blood supply to the area). The patient's hypertension soon disappeared.

It was some fifteen years later that a physician from the Eastern Shore of Maryland was suddenly seized with right lower abdominal pain while returning home from a visit to Baltimore. He was seen by his surgical friend, Dr. William Grose, who believed he did not have appendicitis but that it was safer to explore and see. Nothing abnormal was found and the patient returned home a few days later, only to return in two weeks with florid hypertension. He was believed to be suffering from acute nephritis and was treated accordingly. Within another two weeks, the patient's condition had worsened and he was now in heart failure and almost blind from hemorrhages in his eyes. Because his usual physician was away, Dr. Grose asked me to see him. I could do nothing for the poor fellow but relate to him the story of Dr. Boyd's patient. His response was: "Let's take out my right kidney," which Dr. J. A. C. Colston was loath to do in the face of what was reported to be a normal intravenous pyelogram. But he was persuaded and in process of the right nephrectomy a vein was inadvertently nicked, filling the abdominal cavity with blood. Working hastily, Dr. Colston removed the kidney and handed the bloody mess to me. On washing it with water we were amazed and delighted to find a greyish yellow area exactly like that of Dr. Boyd's patient. Within a week, the hypertension had disappeared. The patient lived for many years, enjoying an active practice.

Dr. Morgan Berthrong, an assistant professor of pathology, examined the kidney and also that of the previous patient. Localized infarction was found in both cases. Knowing that at autopsy many cases were seen each year with similar-appearing lesions but without high blood pressure, Dr. Berthong went further and discovered that these two kidneys inducing hypertension had lesions with incomplete infarctions, i.e., they contained areas with sick but still living kidney cells. Thus was born our interest in high blood pressure from areas in a kidney partially deprived of blood. But how to detect it with more concrete evidence for operation than hunch and guesswork?

As we began to see more such patients, Dr. W. W. Scott and I wondered if some functional change could be found which would disclose the presence of such a lesion. Dr. Scott, therefore, catheterized both kidneys simultaneously in a patient who later proved to have high blood pressure from one kidney, and we examined the urine for every element we could think of, but no differences conspicuous to our eyes were found. However, Dr. Edmund Yendt noted in the Macy Proceedings of a meeting of kidney experts an article by Dr. White, a St. Louis physiologist, in which one renal artery was gradually narrowed and urine from both sides taken simultaneously. Though these experiments were not done for the purpose of studying hypertension, they showed striking reduction in the volume of urine coming from the side with restricted arterial flow and also a decreased concentration of sodium on the same side. On reviewing the findings from Dr. Scott's patient, Yendt noted what we had previously missed—exactly the same findings as White had noted in his experiments—namely, reduced urine flow with decreased concentration of sodium and increased concentration of creatinine on the constricted side. Though requiring expert urological technique and meticulous care in the collection of the urine, the test has proved highly useful to us in predicting the presence of hypertension in cases of stenosis of major renal arteries.

Studies on Urinary Stones

Our active interest in urinary stones really began with the idea that if the mineral content of urine was the only inducer to stone formation, why didn't everyone have stones, since over many years researchers could find no chemical difference in the urine of stone formers than from persons who had never been afflicted with stones. Furthermore, it seemed striking that we had never seen a stone in a patient with renal insufficiency, other than patients infected with urea-splitting organisms. Since all urines contain "chemical products" of calcium and phosphorus far higher than products of those elements which would induce calcification in ricketic cartilage if exhibited in simple saline solution, Dr. William Thomas exposed ricketic cartilage to sterile urine from stone patients and from normal controls. It soon became apparent that most urines from repeated stone formers (calcium oxalate stones) will calcify ricketic rat cartilage, whereas normals will not. Because we, too, as had many others before us, could not distinguish one urine from the other by studying the concentration of chemical constituents, and because dilution and concentration of either type of urine would not alter their attitudes toward calcification of the cartilage, we thought there might be an inhibitor present in non-calcifying urine (which we called "good" urine) and be relatively absent from calcifying urine (termed "evil"). The possibility of substance inhibitory to crystallization was not a new concept. Water chemists have long known of such substances, which are widely used as additives to water supplies for the prevention of calcium carbonate crystals in pipes and boiler ("boiler crud"). The mechanism of action of these water crystal preventers (not softeners), mostly polyphosphates, is not clear. Do they insert themselves into the mass of calcium and carbonate ions as they are about to reach crystalline form and thus prevent the initial minicrystal, or do they adhere to the defect in tiny crystals at which growth occurs and prevent further accretion and aggregation? By a series of physical and chemical steps, we found that the substance we sought to identify in urine was of a very low molecular weight and was highly acidic, and that it operated in our cartilage system almost certainly by preventing crystal *growth*.

Dr. Tak Mukai, a fellow from Japan, was very helpful in these studies. In addition, Dr. John Joule of Manchester, England, came to visit us as a visiting scholar. He made the provocative observation that normal urine brought to pH1 for as little as one minute and then retested at pH7 contained greatly increased inhibitor potential. These concepts were confirmed using artificial urine and noting that tiny quantities of acid greatly potentiated the inhibitor activity.

The Phosphate Story

Coincidence and serendipity surely played roles in the following observations. Dr. William Boyce of Winston-Salem, North Carolina, a renowned student of kidney stone formation, asked my help in securing funds to make a study of phytic acid, a substance derived from the husks of grain. Dr. Douglas Remsen was an old Princeton friend of mine and was working with Squibb & Company, who had a supply of this substance which they agreed to give Boyce for testing. Boyce lived in an area where oxalate stone formers are present in abundance and had patients galore from the mountainous districts of North Carolina. To some thirty of these he doled out quantities of phytic acid at monthly intervals, with a five-dollar bill, asking only that they take the stuff and report back in one month with a twenty-four-hour collection of their urine.

I had taken a very dim view of these experiments; nevertheless, Dr. Boyce invited me to visit Winston-Salem a year later and examine his results with him. To our amazement twenty-eight of the thirty hillbilly subjects reported no change in the number of stones they manufactured, whereas two of them reported complete freedom from stone symptoms.

These two, and these alone, showed enormous increases in phosphate content in their urine. Going to a shelf, we found a chemistry book which showed phosphorus is 85% of the content of phytic acid. I promptly returned to Baltimore and we put three of our patients who had "evil" urine on 1.5 grams of phosphorus per day in the form of Neutra-Phos, which Harry Eisenberg concocted. To our utter amazement the urine of the three patients instantly changed from "evil" to "good." Thus was born Neutra-Phos, which has proven extraordinarily effective in preventing oxalate stones in recurrent stone formers. It was later discovered by Dr. Lynwood Smith, after he had returned to the Mayo Clinic, that everyone who takes the acid will enormously increase his urinary phosphorus, and it became obvious that only two of Boyce's patients had taken their medication, which has a vile taste—the remainder having thrown it down the sink. How the ingestion of added dietary phosphorus increases the quanitity of inhibitor in the urine is not yet known. Adding identical quantities of phosphorus to urine in vitro does not change an "evil" to "good."

Later, working with us but in Dr. Albert Lehninger's Department of Physiological Chemistry, Dr. William Tew, by a very intricate series of steps, isolated phosphocitrate from urine and afterward was able to synthesize it. It seems to be the most potent substance yet known in preventing growth and aggregation of calcific crystals. It has been found in mitochondria, which can contain as much as 30% calcium and phosphorus, and yet not in crystalline form as measured by crystallographic techniques. It is also found in the pancreas of the blue crab, which stores large amounts of calcium and phosphorus in noncrystalline form which it uses to make the new shell after shedding the old one.

Private Practice

In the middle 1930s, the Hopkins decided to demand of its fulltime staff part of their earnings from private patients. This seemed inconsistent to me with the agreement made with the Rockefeller Foundation that the purpose of "full time" was to permit time for teaching and research without the necessity of earning from private practice. Dr. Henry Thomas offered me space in his office, and soon thereafter I was called by Miss Rutherford, Admitting Officer at Hopkins, to ask if I would see a patient who had just arrived from Colombia and wanted an examination. This patient, a charming gentleman, afterward became my close friend and referred innumerable patients from South America, who in turn referred others.

Among the South American patients was a very charming and beautiful lady from Uruguay, who had developed Cushing's syndrome and after adrenalectomy in Montevideo, had become generally pigmented. She was having headaches of nondescript type, no eye changes were seen by the ophthalmologists and she was discharged on the ground that she suffered atypical migrane. Though told not to become pregnant, she did so, and after a normal delivery, the headaches became worse. Partial bilateral hemianopsia was found by her South American doctors and a pituitary tumor was removed. She recovered completely but, of course, still requires corticosteroid replacement which she has periodically sent to her by me. For some reason, in many South American countries the quality of endocrine products purchased is poor. This is true even of thyroid hormone, and patients with hypothyroidism, who should be adequately replaced on their prescribed dosage, have appeared here with blatant myxedema.

It was about this time that Dr. George Thorn had a patient on the clinical research unit which he presented to staff rounds as the "anuric nun." She had gone for days in the unit without any record of passing urine at all and showing no ill effects whatever. When a special nurse was assigned to her room to watch her all night, the patient was forced to confess voiding in the washbasin surreptitiously, much to the chagrin of the physicians who were in charge of her.

Which tale reminds me of another nun, referred to me by Dr. Perry McCullagh of Cleveland. This very beautiful woman had had thyroidectomy for thyrotoxicosis and developed hypoparathyroid tetany thereafter. Despite restoration of the serum calcium to normal with vitamin D, she still had tetany. When I first examined her and applied a tourniquet to do a Trousseau test, I nearly fainted, for the arm to which the tourniquet had been applied remained quiet but the other hand went into carpal spasm. I rushed to the phone and called my friend Dr. Thomas Rennie, on the psychiatric staff, to come over quickly and treat either the nun or me. He promptly transferred her to the psychiatric unit, where it later was found that she had been having an affair with a priest. This lady was followed by us for many years thereafter but continued to be beset with medical problems and eventually died of hypertension and kidney failure. My nerves eventually recovered from this startling episode.

There had been a huge hue and cry in the papers by the anti-vivisectionists about cruelty to dogs and other animals by Hopkins experimenters. Dr. Chesney actively campaigned against interference and asked my help with Mr. Jack Pollack, then a bigwig boss in Baltimore politics. Mr. Pollack's daughter was a patient of mine, suffering from diabetes. I went to see Mr. Pollack at Dr. Chesney's request and, after explaining the situation, was assured there would be no problem with the City Council. Mr. Pollack was as good as his word and the bill was convincingly defeated to everyone's relief.

In 1958 I went to the CIBA Foundation conference in London, aboard the *S.S. United States*. The President of the line was a patient and friend and I went in great style and with special attention. On board was Dr. Milton Eisenhower, taking his daughter to Europe for a vacation, having just lost his wife. We were introduced at the captain's cocktail party and Dr. Eisenhower, who was already being sounded out for the presidency of Johns Hopkins, quizzed me about Baltimore and Hopkins in particular. Being only a minor operator at Hopkins, I could not answer many of his questions, but found him a most charming man, as I did subsequently when he accepted the invitation to Hopkins.

We also on this trip had the privilege of being shown Land's End by Sir Henry Dale.

Personal Medical Problems

Throughout all these years I had continued to play tennis regularly, though not as well as previously. But my tennis days ended abruptly when I awakened one morning with pain in the right shoulder and during the day a subcutaneous hemorrhage became evident which extended all the way to the wrist where it stopped abruptly. The orthopedic consultant felt that I had ruptured the right shoulder capsule and wanted to inject dye to see where the tear had occurred. But on being told that if the tear were repaired I had only a 50% chance of having a good shoulder and that I should expect to have many weeks with the arm in a cast, the odds seemed to me too poor to suffer them. Some weeks later the correct diagnosis became obvious; the orthopedist noted that the inner head of the biceps had ruptured, being now completely atrophied and too late for operative intervention.

A year or so after the above episode, while driving to the hospital one morning, I became aware of an unpleasant sensation beneath my breastbone. A house officer, noting my appearance, immediately conducted me to the outpatient cardiographic laboratory where a coronary occlusion was diagnosed and I was escorted to the Coronary Care Unit. Here it became apparent that there was much difference being on the receiving and giving end of medical attention. After being examined by several members of the house staff, a fourth examiner finally came in. She was a gynecologist on leave from Columbia University in New York to study acute emergency medicine. After a very perfunctory examination she reported hearing moisture in my lungs, whereas when asked to take a deep breath I had merely gone through the motions of breathing without transferring any air into or out of my lungs. I think her responsibilities on the unit ceased thereafter.

An amusing episode happened during my brief stay in the Coronary Care Unit. I was hooked up to an electrocardiograph, which registered above my bed and was thus visible to me as well as another recording at the nurses' station. In the middle of the night I rang the bell and was answered promptly by the nurse to know what she could do. My reply was that my heart had stopped beating, according to the recording above my bed. With some chagrin she replied, "So it has," and promptly came to my bedside and found that the chest "lead" had fallen off my chest and when this was replaced, the cardiographic recording promptly resumed.

There are recollections of other incidents along the way perhaps worthy of mention. At a meeting of the Association of American Physicians in the 1940s, an unusual and amusing incident occurred. Usually these meetings are the essence of dignity. At this one, Dr. Russell Wilder of the Mayo Clinic gave a talk on why parathyroid adenomas did not occur in Rochester, Minnesota. He blamed it on the quality of the air and the water and the beer. The talk was really rather ridiculous and Fuller Albright rose to comment as follows: "It seems strange that the Massachusetts General has now had some fifty instances of parathyroid adenoma, and yet the Boston City Hospital, with the same air and water and only a few blocks away, has had none." There was laughter. After the meeting, Dr. Harrop asked me to join him with Dr. Wilder and several others for a Brighton punch. Dr. Harrop was in a glum mood for he had just been notified that the presidency of the Endocrine Society, to which he had been elected, had been withdrawn since he was leaving academic medicine to join Squibb & Company. Dr. Harrop asked Dr. Wilder why he had given the paper on parathyroid adenomas and was told that Charlie Mayo had ordered it, being disgruntled that so many cases were being seen in Boston and Baltimore and none at the Mayo Clinic.

There was the lovely banquet in San Francisco where I was given the Passano Award, introductory remarks being given by Sam Asper. It was a gala affair, attended by my wife, my daughter, my son James and his wife Nancy, and my long-standing secretary, Miss Eleanor Fry.

I was also invited to give the Farquharson Memorial Lecture at the Royal College of Medicine in Toronto. In the invitation it stated that a cap and gown should be worn, that the presentation of the award would be carried out by Lord so-and-so. I became worried about what I should say in reply, but reading further was the welcome cryptic statement, "There will be no opportunity for rebuttal."

The Connell Lecture in Queen's University at Kingston, Ontario was another most pleasant occasion. I recall no unusual incidents, but at a staff conference I was presented with an Indian girl whom I had seen five years previously at Toronto with phosphate diabetes. She had had a five-year interval with freedom from bone pain but had returned to Dr. Yendt with bone pains which she said were different. There was a bandage on her neck and this time she had had a parathyroid adenoma removed. This was the first instance in my experience for a patient with phosphate diabetes to have later developed hyperparathyroidism. Whether the parathyroidism was brought on by the phosphate and vitamin D treatment of the phosphate diabetes is not known, but the same sequence of events has since been reported several times.

Another incident that remains clear in my mind relates to the International Congress on Endocrinology held in Copenhagen. Since I was President of the Endocrine Society at the time, I was invited to preside at one of the plenary sessions. My wife, daughter and I had gone to England preceding the meeting and toured England and Scotland. A reservation had been made for me to take a boat from Newcastle, England to the Hook of Holland, and my wife and daughter escorted me to the boat. At the boat I found no reservation but was told I could sleep in the crowded saloon with many others. After looking about, the prosect did not please me, so I debarked but without reporting my debarkation to Customs. We drove on to London where some days later we finally did get reservations to get to Holland. But on arrival in Holland, I was at first refused entry because my passport read that I was already in Holland. After much haggling and explaining, a kindly immigration officer finally admitted me but I was too late for the Congress. We then continued our tour and drove along the Weser River into Luxembourg and then into France. The car we were driving had been rented from a Hamburg company and thus was supplied with German licenses. The Danes did not like Germans then and I doubt do now.

In any event, my wife and daughter were refused admission to the ladies room at the gasoline station on one occasion because we were thought to be German. On arrival at the dock where we were to embark for homeward passage, a representative of the Hamburg renting company was supposed to meet me to take back his car but he never showed up so I simply left the car with the keys in it on the dock and never heard how that all worked out. The company here that arranged our trip caused us much embarrassment by its bungling and I won't mention the name for fear of a libel suit but, needless to say, we dealt no further with them.

Guy's Hospital

In 1952, Dr. W. W. Scott and I were selected to go to London on the Johns Hopkins-Guy's Hospital exchange. My daughter Lucy, my wife and I boarded a small Cunard steamship along with the Scotts. My daughter became seasick before we got out of New York Harbor. There was good reason to be seasick later in the passage and my daughter remained below decks most of the time. Dr. Scott and I spent several pleasant evenings with the ship's officers and I was for the first time introduced to Guinness Stout, which the ship's captain felt to be a better antidote for *mal de mer* than was champagne, as most Americans believed.

Soon after my arrival at Guy's Hospital, Dr. Kenneth McLean, who had been assigned to visit with me, was called to the emergency room to see a very ill patient whom he had never seen before. The man was comatose with a very stiff neck and obviously was suffering from meningitis. But the spinal fluid contained no white blood cells at all. We reasoned that he had no white cells to get into the spinal fluid and this proved to be the case, he having total agranulocytosis. At autopsy the pathologist, Mr. Simpson, also a famous forensic pathologist, was so impressed with this reasoning that he subsequently asked me to give several clinical pathological conferences with him. It was later found that our patient was being treated for syphilis with arsphenamine, which was the culprit for having knocked out his granulocytes, leaving him with no resistance to the organisms in his brain and spinal fluid.

During our London stay, through the kindness of friends on the *Baltimore Sun*, their affiliate, the *Manchester Guardian*, had arranged for us to go to the Houses of Parliament and witness the debate, followed by luncheon there. To show my appreciation for their kindness, I arranged to have a mint julep party at the *Guardian's* office on Fleet Street. All went well, but the next morning's paper had an editorial in which the party was described: "The juleps would have been okay had they not been so cold, and they could have done without the spinach stuck in them."

Dr. Max Rosenheim, a famous English clinician who was very kind to us while we were on the Guy's exchange, was visiting us at our home in the early 1950s and was making ward rounds with Dr. Harvey when he became afflicted with severe chest pain. Dr. Harvey had an electrocardiogram done which proved normal, and he summoned me to his office where I found Dr. Rosenheim pale, sweating and much alarmed. When I applied my stethoscope to his chest he winced visibly and the diagnosis of Tietze's syndrome became obvious (inflammation of the costochondral junction and sternum of unknown cause). The symptoms soon passed and Dr. Rosenheim resumed his usual duties. He attended with us the Maryland Hunt Cup steeplechase race and afterward went with us to Dr. Baetjer's mint julep party, where he was introduced to this luscious beverage.

While at Guy's Hospital, the then-Dean Dr. Boland (late Sir Rowan Boland) and his wife were most hospitable and invited us on occasion to their home in Kent for weekends. Thus, when Dr. Boland became exchange visitor to Hopkins, they were invited out to our house for a weekend. Dr. Boland promptly became ill with the flu and ran a high fever, all the more alarming since he had earlier had pulmonary tuberculosis. He stayed for two weeks. Our ancient black butler, Henry, had a cantankerous nature, and we wondered how he and the English physician would get on, but they took to one another like ducks to water. Every afternoon, Henry would bring tea and cinnamon toast to Dr. Boland's room. The flu finally wore itself out, and Dr. Boland completely recovered, but it was a very trying and worrisome experience, especially for Mrs. Boland.

On my second trip to England some years later, the Professor of Urology at Guy's Hospital, Mr. George Doherty, was most kind to me, inviting me to be a guest in his luxurious home adjacent to Guy's Hospital for a week of my stay. It was the only time in my life ever to be served by "Jeeves." I was awakened in the morning to find a bath drawn, my clothes laid out and tea with two newspapers at my bedside. I was very popular at Guy's for I had four tickets to Wimbledon which then, as now, are frightfully difficult to come by.

When Mr. George Doherty subsequently came to Baltimore on the exchange, we invited him and his wife to our home for the weekend. It was summertime and terribly hot, which Englishmen tolerate poorly. During Saturday afternoon they spent their time lying on the lawn while Lucy and James, my son, mowed the hay field with a tractor. After this we gave a rather elaborate dinner party, having as guests the Carlyle Bartons, Dr. Baetjer and several other bigwigs. Lucy carried this off with such aplomb that I am told this was why she was invited to become a member of the Baltimore Assembly Committee and later to be its Chairman, the epitome of social prestige in the city.

We did not often entertain such fancy folks but on another occasion did invite Dr. and Mrs. Bowman to dinner along with several trustees of my age, who were close friends. Dr. Bowman, President of the University, arrived half an hour late and, when offered a cocktail, requested ginger ale instead. He then went into a very boring explanation stating that a cocktail kept him awake at night. Dr. Baetjer become more and more restless during this harangue and finally burst out with: "Mr. Bowman, have you ever tried drinking two or three?" Dr. Bowman, not the least abashed, continued talking and monopolizing the conversation all during the dinner.

My mother-in-law was a severe asthmatic. Dr. Baetjer supplied her with morphine to be taken hypodermically when attacks became severe. One evening I was called by her nurse (she lived just across the road) to come at once, that Mrs. Iglehart was very ill. When I arrived Mrs. Iglehart lay comatose and not breathing at all. I administered artificial respiration and soon Dr. Walter Baetjer and Dr. Warde Allan arrived to spell me, but during one of my turns, quite a few minutes later, Mrs. Iglehart suddenly roused and demanded in angry terms to know what I thought I was doing. Whether the nurse had given an overdose of medicine or not we never knew, but Mrs. Iglehart seemed perfectly all right and lived for many years afterward.

In the late 1940s, I was custodian for the ACTH, which Armour & Company was supplying for experimental use, when two remarkable experiences occurred. A Hopkins nurse, with asthma so severe she had to be given rectal ether to sleep, was admitted by Dr. Walter Winkenwerder to have nasal polyps removed by Dr. John Bordley in the hope of alleviating her asthma. She was given ACTH one evening and met me the next morning walking in the corridor, a thing she had not been able to do for many months. Later that morning Dr. Bordley phoned me asking what we had done, for her polyps had disappeared. Continuing small doses of ACTH, this remarkable woman was able to resume her nursing duties.

I pursuaded my mother-in-law, who was a chronic sufferer from asthma, to let me give her some ACTH. The effects were dramatic and her breathing was completely relieved but after a few days she refused to take any more ACTH because, and her expression was, "It makes my brain feel like mashed potatoes." I never understood just what this feeling was, but to my amazement several patients who had taken ACTH for various reasons used the same terms as had Mrs. Iglehart, namely that the brain felt like mashed potatoes.

A middle-aged diabetic who also had chronic lymphatic leukemia was referred to me in severe ketoacidosis. It required over 1000 units of insulin plus sodium bicarbonate daily to keep his chemical picture near normal. After four days of ACTH, he no longer required insulin. A product very antagonistic to insulin was found in his serum by Dr. George Mirick and Dr. Stadie of Philadelphia verified this, using his diaphragm uptake test for accumulations of glucose in vitro.

Insulin activity in any mixture could be assayed by this method. A very high titer against insulin was found by both these techniques. The insulin resistance had disappeared by the twentieth day. When these observations were reported in Chicago at an Armour & Company-sponsored meeting, they were greeted with incredulity. The patient lived many years with his leukemia, and his diabetes was controlled with diet alone. Whether or not his leukemia cells were cloned to make insulin antibodies, we, of course, never knew. But his high lymphocyte count did not change with the improvement in diabetic management.

Hurricanes

We were visiting my mother-in-law in Northeast Harbor, Maine, when one afternoon I went over to the Kimball House to collect the mail. We were wont to have cocktails about 6:00 P.M. and always had them with Mrs. Iglehart in her room. Mr. Kimball had informed me that there was a hurricane on the way. On being told this news, Mrs. Iglehart promptly said "Goodness, let us have cocktails right away." Ever since then, when told of a sudden catastrophe, those in the family are likely to say, "Heavens, let us have cocktails right away."

We had many wonderful cruises while at Northeast Harbor. At first we rented boats and took along a skipper (captain). Generally we headed east, because it was less likely that we would run into other cruisers and the country was wilder. On one such cruise, accompanied by Dr. Oliver Cope, Samuel Morison, the author of *Naval History of World War II*, Dr. Myles Baker and Dr. Richard Shackelford, we headed west, being warned of a severe hurricane which was then around Martha's Vineyard but headed straight for Maine. On arrival at Burnt Coat on Forbes Island, we went on up into the Inner Harbor (Burnt Coat) and inquired of the lobstermen where it would be advisable for us to batten down for the night. Having gained the desired information, we returned to Forbes Island, for the radio reported that the storm had moved off Martha's Vineyard and would not strike Maine. However, while Morison was cooking supper and Baker and I were taking a shower in the pouring rain, there was a crack of thunder like a pistol shot. Winds struck us in full force and our tender rope had snapped. Hurriedly we started the engines and with only the bare poles upright, headed directly into the wind for Burnt Coat Harbor. It took us an hour to run the mile into the harbor, so fierce was the wind. We spent the night peeking out of portholes to see if we were dragging, but we weren't, and by 5:00 A.M. things calmed down a bit.

We sailed back down to Forbes Island, then occupied by a group of Harvard students who had seen what happened and rescued our tender for us. We went out the back passage and, on a long reach with a forty-knot wind, sailed east up the Coast, almost reaching Rocque Island by evening. It was a fantastic experience but without fright because Cope and our captain were such superb sailors. That hurricane did not blow itself out for several days and we subsequently had some more narrow escapes.

On another cruise we were fogged in at the Cow Yard and Cope and I had been overboard for a swim in icy water. On climbing back aboard, we shouted to Dr. John Enders of Nobel fame (for his part in the poliomyelitis vaccine), who was below deck not having swum with us, to hurry up and bring us cocktails. Enders's voice from below: "I can call spirits from the vasty deep, aye, so can any man, but when you call them, will they come?" I later looked this up and the quotation was exact from Shakespeare's *Henry IV*.

On another occasion, Enders was with us on a cruise, this time to our later regret. We were holed up by fog in the little back harbor on Rocque Island; Cope and I had gone out to dig some clams. On our return, Enders was in his bunk with cough and fever. He told us he had been playing with one of his cold viruses before leaving Boston and that this particular one had a five-day incubation period, and we would all come down with it the following Tuesday. We reached home port that Sunday evening and all the crew headed homeward. Sure enough, all but two came down with Enders's symptoms Tuesday morning.

Trip to Mexico

Dr. Robert Johnston, whose son was a Fellow with us, invited Lucy and me on a trip with him and his wife to Mexico. We started in Houston in the Johnston's Cadillac and drove to Laredo, Texas, where we crossed the border to have a dinner of doves, the most I had ever eaten. Dr. Johnston, an obstetrician, had been present at the birth of every prominent Houston citizen for many years, and many in South America. He had been invited to give a talk in Mexico City to the Medical Society, and so I was roped in to give a talk, too. Mine was on hypertension from ischemia of one kidney. The talks went okay and the Mexican doctors outdid themselves in hospitality. Here I was taken to my only exhibition of a bullfight, after barely having recovered from a most disagreeable attack of *"tourista."*

But what I remember most about the trip was the terror struck in one's heart by Mrs. Johnston's driving the car around the curves on the roads from Monterey to Mexico City, looking down a thousand feet with no guard rails. This was especially perilous since Mrs. Johnston enjoyed her cocktails, sometimes a bit much. Dr. Johnston, too, had his quirks and insisted that we were on the right road whenever he saw signs saying *"Non Estamenda"* which, of course, meant "No Parking." On one occasion, we were at a gas station where a little man who thought he had been defrauded—common enough—asked Dr. Johnston for assistance in remonstrating with the gas station attendant. Dr. Johnston, who had a deep Southern drawl, waved the man aside with the remark, "I don't speak Spanish." "I don't either," replied the man, "I am from North Dakota."

During my early years of practice, an event occurred which upset our household for several days. At about 6:00 A.M., a car drove into our driveway with much horn blowing. It awakened our sons, who rushed to the front door to find a friend announcing that his wife was in the car having a baby. Jimmy got me out of bed, his hair literally standing straight up, and urged me to come down instantly, which I did, not even waiting to put on a bathrobe. The baby had already arrived. I called my wife to get a flannel blanket and I went to the kitchen where our ancient cook was making rolls for breakfast and demanded a sharp knife and some string because a baby was being born in a car at the front door. "Go along and leave me to my bread," was her reply. "Why don't folks have babies at home like they used to?"

I tied the umbilical cord and then cut it, went back inside and handed the baby to my wife, who was terrified. I told her to swab out the baby's mouth and wrap the infant in a flannel blanket, and then phoned the obstetrician, who started to give me lengthy instructions on how to proceed. But I told him to meet me at Women's Hospital, and that I would bring mother and child right in. We were met at the door by the head nurse, who had formerly been at Hopkins, and who knew me well. "You have changed your specialty," she remarked on being handed the baby. The obstetrician soon arrived and all was well.

A sequel to the story is that my friend, Mr. Charles Garland, was giving a large luncheon that day before the Yale-Navy football game. On my entry to the Garlands, I was greeted by Dr. Detlov Bronk, then President of Johns Hopkins University, with the remark, "I have just changed your title to Professor of Obstetrics." News travels fast.

My first talk at the Association of American Physicians was delivered last on the program on a Wednesday afternoon. There were only two listeners—the President and the recorder. After the talk, Dr. Woodyatt, the President, comforted me by saying he had enjoyed it—sweet words from a gallant gentleman.

Just this past summer my cup was again filled to overflowing when a library of Endocrinology, at Johns Hopkins, was dedicated in my honor. The affair was very elaborate, with many friends and former fellow workers coming from far and wide, many of them giving speeches which were embarrassingly flattering. A wine and cheese party followed and then a tour of the new library, which contained many of my memorabilia, including a portrait.

I should be remiss if credit were not given to the several ladies most influential in aiding and abetting me through these interesting paths. First and foremost, of course, my ever-patient wife, who calmly suffered the dreariness and loneliness of many days, as has nearly every other physician's wife, much less that of a pseudo-scientist; also to my mother, who was always kindly, loving and fair; my secretary of some forty-four years, Miss Eleanor Fry, who suffered my eccentricities and frequent errors with such patience and loyalty; also some of my lady canine friends who have ever been companionable and consolingly patient. I was also blessed with a mother-in-law who was generous to a fault. And many lady patients who have remained loyal despite some of my bumbling efforts and periods of grouchiness.

Changes in Johns Hopkins and Baltimore

It is not an easy task, in one's waning years, to compare the state of affairs today with those of his youth. Thus, an effort to compare Baltimore and the Johns Hopkins Medical Institutions now and in the 1920s is inevitably laden with biases of one sort or another. It is easier for this octogenarian to see changes in the Johns Hopkins than in his native city.

The physical changes in the north Broadway institutions are tremendous. When I was a house officer at Johns Hopkins, the assistant resident physicians were provided sleeping quarters on the second floor of the administration building, above the statue of Christ. Though work and sleep occupied most of the time spent there, there was also a gay camaraderie that I suspect is lacking today, or at least it seems so to me. Of a nighttime, Dr. Edmund Kelly, son of the famous gynecologist, was one of the most lighthearted, and always took himself to bed with a leap and a loud "Look out, Morpheus, here comes Kelly." It was he who conceived the idea of having a turtle race, which has since reached enormous proportions and with urban publicity.

I spent little time in my room in the adminstration building, having been married and occupying a house on Wolfe Street, then highly respectable. We were not fearful of attack by day or night and freely roamed the neighborhood. When, as students on the obstetrical service, we walked in the middle of the night with a nurse to attend births, with little fear of abuse, and usually with a warm welcome by the family of the expectant patient.

In the years of my house-officership and early years as a visiting physician, the doctors' dining room was situated just off the main corridor of the hospital north and east of the Marburg building. Here convened the house staff and visiting physicians. At lunch, there was a large, long table occupied by the senior staff members, and it was a fortunate occasion to be invited by one of the bigwigs to join him at that table. The rest of the staff ate at small round tables for eight or ten. All were served, and as I recall it, a far more respectable meal could be had than is available today at the cafeteria-style dining room where one sits catch as catch can, and pays exorbitant prices for very mediocre food. Fifty years ago there was much more commingling of house staff and upper visiting staff, resulting in much greater camaraderie. We looked up to our seniors with friendly awe and were generally treated with friendliness and respect. Today, the attitude of house staff members to visiting physicians seems different in the main, though far better than ten or twenty years ago. At that time the students and house staff took a very cantankerous attitude, behaving often as if they were doing us a favor to be taught. This attitude has changed back for the better recently, and I believe that has been generally true all around the country.

During visits on the wards, even now, the resident physicians frequently do not attend rounds, claiming they have so much paper work to do that they do not have the time. This attitude reflects down to the interns and students, who seem to gain the inference that rounds with attending physicians can mean but little to their advancement. The enormous advances in medical technology plays some part in this separation of lower staff from the upper. One finds that before a student or house officer ever sees the patient he is supplied by an automated list of laboratory reports, including x-rays; hence he feels that history and physical examination are perfunctory tasks, obsolete by advances in modern technology. Furthermore, the young doctor feels that he knows far more about interpretation of chemical data supplied to him by tests than does his preceptor, as this is unfortunately often the case. Efforts are being made to change all this and hopefully they will be successful.

As to changes in Baltimore, as a member of a family which has been here for many generations I can see little different except the physical. Downtown is totally different and I scarcely know my way around. But the Mt. Vernon place remains as I remember it as a boy, only one block from where we lived at 209 West Monument Street.

Baltimore's friendliness and hospitality remain unchanged if one has the entrée. But this is true of most other cities as well, at least we have found it so in Boston, Philadelphia and Chicago. Most members of families that have lived for long periods in Baltimore rarely dine out in restaurants, preferring to have meals at home or at the homes of friends or, barring that, at a club. But the standard of living is vastly different. The chauffeur, commonplace in my youth, is now a vanishing breed, and live-in house servants are a rarity. One walks the streets warily, even in the elite suburbs, and few wives will remain at the Mt. Vernon Club after 4 P.M. The dangers around the Johns Hopkins Hospital are widely known, and local patients are reluctant to be there because their friends and relatives fear to visit them. Muggings and rapes around the hospital have been commonplace stories for the press, despite efforts of Pinkerton and other guards to prevent them. One is asked for identification to enter the hospital, even after having worked there for fifty years. And since one wears a white butcher's coat while at work, it is a nuisance to transfer an I.D. card from one's pocket back to the white coat on arrival each day.

The great riots after Martin Luther King's shooting are still vivid memories. I recall the night the rioting began. I was in Boston attending an Interurban Club meeting, and after dinner at the Tavern Club I sought a taxi. After walking several blocks, a friendly Irish policeman hailed a cab for me and over the driver's remonstrances ordered him to take me to South Station to catch the Federal Express home. The trip in the taxi proved uneventful, though there were policemen in evidence all along the route. Sunday morning, after arrival in Baltimore and a trip home for breakfast, I went to the hospital to see a sick patient. I was the last person to get down Broadway unharmed. Dr. Murray Fisher had a brick thrown through his car window and received minor injuries, but several other doctors on their way received more serious damage. After that, the Army was called in, and there were guns placed at North Avenue facing south and guns at Monument Street facing north. Those were dangerous and ugly days in Baltimore. Things have calmed down considerably since those tempestuous days, though perhaps interrelations are still not what one would like them to be.

But from a broad overview of the mores of Baltimore, one might say of it as one does of Paris, "The more it changes the more it remains the same."